KING LEAR, MACBETH,
INDEFINITION, AND TRAGEDY

KING LEAR, MACBETH, INDEFINITION, AND TRAGEDY

Stephen Booth

Yale University Press
New Haven and London

Designed by Nancy Ovedovitz and set in Garamond No. 3 type by
Northeast Typographic Services, Meriden, Connecticut. Printed in
the United States of America by Edwards Brothers Inc., Ann Arbor,
Michigan.

Library of Congress Cataloging in Publication Data
Booth, Stephen.
   King Lear, Macbeth, indefinition, and tragedy.
   Includes index.
   1. Shakespeare, William, 1564–1616—Tragedies. 2. Shake-
speare, William, 1564–1616. King Lear. 3. Shakespeare, William,
1564–1616. Macbeth. 4. Tragedy. I. Title. II. Title: Indefinition
and tragedy.
PR2983.B6   1983   822.3′3   83-42875
ISBN 0–300–02850-4

10   9   8   7   6   5   4   3   2   1

For
Josephine Miles

CONTENTS

Preface   ix

PART I

ON THE GREATNESS OF *KING LEAR*   1

1 The Promised End   5
2 Something More to Say   11
3 Identity and Definition   20
4 Altogether Fool   33
5 Inconclusion   43

INTERLUDE
LIKENESSES AND DIFFERENCES BETWEEN
LOVE'S LABOR'S LOST AND
KING LEAR, COMEDY AND TRAGEDY   59

PART II

MACBETH, ARISTOTLE, DEFINITION, AND TRAGEDY   79

1 Hold Enough   81
2 Fair Is Foul, and Foul Is Fair   105

APPENDIX 1
ON THE PERSISTENCE OF FIRST IMPRESSIONS   119

APPENDIX 2
SPECULATIONS ON DOUBLING IN
SHAKESPEARE'S PLAYS   127

Notes   157
Index   179

PREFACE

Whatever they ought rightly to be, prefaces are often minimally disguised apologia in which authors attempt to disarm predictable criticisms of their books. In extreme cases, prefaces explain why the books in behalf of which they insinuate are as they are and are not as their authors have good reason to expect their readers would rather they be. This is an extreme case.

The two essays that are this book's core propound that same idea: the response we record when we label an event tragic is a response to the fact of indefinition. Each also propounds the related idea that literary works we call tragedies have their value as enabling actions by which we are made capable, temporarily, of enduring manifestations of the fact that nothing in human experience is or can be definite. The two essays, however, go at their common concern differently. The one on *King Lear* is just that: an essay on that particular tragedy. The other one, as its title suggests, starts from the idea of tragedy—in particular, from an idea that emerged from my thinking about *Lear,* the idea about the inherent connection between tragedy and desire for definition—and presents *Macbeth* in support of it.

Unfortunately, the foregoing paragraph makes the book sound considerably neater than it is. The essays printed here are formally independent of one another. The form the book takes is the form in which it evolved. In saying that, I do not mean to suggest there is virtue in recording one's thinking in a way that approximates the haphazard order in which it occurs. Yet to have reworked the materials of this book in such a way as to give them linear coherence would have required the fabrication of an ideational superstructure for the sake of achieving a formal one. To fabricate such a superstructure would have been to divert the book's energy to—and focus its reader's attention on—an extensive mechanism generated for its own sake. I did not want that to happen.

I should, I think, comment specifically on what I say in Part II about Aristotle's *Poetics.* The first part of the *Macbeth* essay has been taken to be an attack on Aristotle or on Aristotelian critics. I am not out to "debunk" Aristotle, and I take pains to say so in the essay. Nonetheless, audiences to whom I have read drafts of the essay persist in referring to my "assault on Aristotle," and students who have read the essay in manuscript persist in prefacing their comments with "I know you hate Aristotle, but . . ." Since my prose seems to have failed me in the essay proper, let me anticipate reactions by stating here that my aim in pages 81−90 is not to say that the emperor has no clothes but to point out that he has a beautiful body.

Excerpts from Part I appeared in *Twentieth Century Interpretations of King Lear,* ed. Janet Adelman (Englewood Cliffs, N.J.: Prentice Hall, 1978), and a version of Appendix 2 was previously published in *Shakespeare: The Theatrical Dimension,* ed. Philip C. McGuire and David A. Samuelson (New York: AMS Press, 1979).

Except where I specifically say otherwise, all line references to Shakespeare's works are to the Revised Pelican Text, ed. Alfred Harbage et al. (Baltimore, 1969).

This book has been a long time in the making. I have worked on it intermittently over several years during which I began and finished other projects. I began the book on a Guggenheim Fellowship more than ten years ago. I was and remain grateful, and I am very much relieved to be able at last to show the Guggenheim Foundation that I spent 1970−71 doing something besides spend its money. The costs of typing the manuscript were paid from research funds provided by the University of California, Berkeley, and, latterly, by the University of Hawaii, where I am currently visiting; I am grateful to both institutions.

I am also grateful to Nancy Laleau and Kathleen Kenny Hirsh for bibliographical assistance; to several of my past and present Berkeley colleagues for criticism and advice (notably, to Janet Adelman, to Wayne Shumaker, to Laurence Jacobs, to Ulrich Knoepflmacher, to King-Kok Cheung, and—most particularly—to Judith Radner, who read the whole manuscript with a combination of painful care and large-minded wisdom that few other people are either able or generous enough to have provided); to David Rabey for moral support sufficient to have sustained the Tay Bridge; and to Ellen Graham, my editor at the Yale University Press, for her kindness, her wisdom, her tact, and her undoubtedly excessive patience.

Throughout this book's prolonged and complicated gestation, my wife has been her usual superlative self. However—or, probably, moreover—she strongly advised me to change the book's title. She finds it confusing and potentially misleading. She fears (I think unnecessarily), that its four listed ingredients will be mistaken for appositive pairs and that people will fancy me to be presenting *King Lear*—an example of indefinition—as the first in a *contrasting* pair with *Macbeth*—an example of tragedy *as opposed to* indefinition. Although I chose to disregard her advice about the title, it is nonetheless possible that, in this sole instance, I was not altogether foolish to do so. Her name is Susan Patek Booth.

S. B.

Honolulu, Hawaii
September 6, 1982

PART I
ON THE GREATNESS
OF *KING LEAR*

The Get-Ready Man was a lank unkempt elderly gentleman with wild eyes and a deep voice who used to go about shouting at people through a megaphone to prepare for the end of the world. "GET READY! GET READ-Y!" he would bellow. "THE WORLLLD IS COMING TO AN END!" His startling exhortations would come up, like summer thunder, at the most unexpected times and in the most surprising places. I remember once during Mantell's production of "King Lear" at the Colonial Theatre, that the Get-Ready Man added his bawlings to the squealing of Edgar and the ranting of the King and the mouthing of the Fool, rising from somewhere in the balcony to join in. The theatre was in absolute darkness and there were rumblings of thunder and flashes of lightning offstage. Neither father nor I, who were there, ever completely got over the scene, which went something like this:

Edgar: Tom's a-cold. —O, do de, do de, do de! —Bless thee from whirlwinds, star-blasting, and taking . . . the foul fiend vexes! (Thunder off.

Lear: What! Have his daughters brought him to this pass? —

Get-Ready Man: Get ready! Get ready!

Edgar: Pillicock sat on Pillicock-hill:—Halloo, halloo, loo, loo!

(Lightning flashes.

Get-Ready Man: The Worllld is com-ing to an End!

Fool: This cold night will turn us all to fools and madmen!

Edgar: Take heed o' the foul fiend: obey thy paren—

Get-Ready Man: Get rea-dy!

Edgar: Tom's a-cold!

Get-Ready Man: The Worr-uld is coming to an end! . . .

They found him finally, and ejected him, still shouting. The Theatre, in our time, has known few such moments.

—*James Thurber, from "The Car We Had to Push" in* My Life and Hard Times

In King Lear *everything tends toward a conclusion that does not occur; even personal death, for Lear, is terribly delayed. Beyond the apparent worst there is a worse suffering, and when the end comes it is not only more appalling than anybody expected, but a mere image of that horror, not the thing itself. The end is now a matter of immanence; tragedy assumes the figurations of apocalypse, of death and judgement, heaven and hell; but the world goes forward in the hands of exhausted survivors. Edgar haplessly assumes the dignity; only the king's natural body is at rest. This is the tragedy of sempiternity; apocalypse is translated out of time into the* aevum. *The world may, as Gloucester supposes, exhibit all the symptoms of decay and change, all the terrors of an approaching end, but when the end comes it is not an end, and both suffering and the need for patience are perpetual.*

—Frank Kermode, from The
Sense of an Ending

1. *The Promised End*

The tragedy of Lear, deservedly celebrated among the dramas of Shakespeare, is commonly regarded as his greatest achievement. I submit that *King Lear* is so because it is the greatest achievement of his audience, an audience of theatrically unaccommodated men. If an audience's achievement in surviving the harrowing experience of *King Lear* could ever reasonably have been doubted, it has been taken for granted since this superbly forthright note on *King Lear* in Samuel Johnson's edition of Shakespeare: "I was many years ago so shocked by Cordelia's death, that I know not whether I ever endured to read again the last scenes of the play till I undertook to revise them as an editor."[1] If my sensations could add anything to Johnson's, I might relate that I myself first read the last scenes of *King Lear* while undergoing a sophomore survey course in which I was taking on a full semester's reading in the twenty-four hours immediately preceding the final examination; it was about three o'clock on a spring afternoon, and I sat in a chair in a stuffy library and cried. I had already read a pound and a half of certified masterpieces that day; I read as much more before dawn; but with this one exception I was moved by nothing beyond the sophomoric ambition to become a junior. Further testimony to the singular power of the last scenes of *King Lear* is presumably unnecessary. An effort to account for that singularity may well seem just as unnecessary, but I think the reasons why we are so upset by the end of *Lear*—specifically by the death of Cordelia—appear to be more obvious than they are.

The context in which Johnson introduces his personal response suggests that his distress was ethical; Johnson took Shakespeare's purpose to be

> to impress this important moral, that villany is *never at a stop,* that crimes lead to crimes, and *at last terminate* in ruin.

> But though this moral be incidentally enforced, Shakespeare has suffered the virtue of Cordelia to perish in a just cause, contrary to the natural ideas of justice, to the hope of the reader, and, what is yet more strange, to the faith of chronicles. . . . A play in which the wicked prosper, and the virtuous miscarry, may doubtless be good, because it

5

is a just representation of the common events of human life: but since all reasonable beings naturally love justice, I cannot easily be persuaded, that the observation of justice makes a play worse; or, that if other excellencies are equal, the audience will not always rise better pleased from the final triumph of persecuted virtue.

In the present case the publick has decided. Cordelia, from the time of Tate, has always retired with victory and felicity. [VIII, 704; the italics are mine]

Disappointment of our hopes and of our natural ideas of justice accounts handsomely for our shock at Cordelia's death; that explanation makes perfect sense. But—in the unlikely event that *King Lear* has anything to teach us—it may be the necessity of recognizing that what makes sense may not be true. Literature abounds in instances in which virtue miscarries—Little Eva, Little Nell, Little Emily, little Macduff, the little princes in the Tower—but, though we may be moved by disasters that befall innocents, our emotion does not ordinarily spill over into terror at the works that contain those disasters. If the power and intensity of our responses to the last moments of *King Lear* do not result from *what* happens, they may result from *when* and *where* it happens.

These are the last words of Act IV; the speaker is Kent: "My point and period will be thoroughly wrought, / Or well and ill, as this day's battle's fought" (IV.vii.96−97). This speech—which functions similarly to similar ones in *Julius Caesar* (V.i.112−25), *Othello* (V.i.128−29), and *Macbeth* (V.iv.16−21)—virtually announces something the play has been telling us for over an hour: as Dover has been the destination of the characters, the inevitable battle there is the destination of the play.

At the beginning of V.iii, the last scene, that battle is over, and Lear and Cordelia are led away as captives; they are in urgent danger of death at the hands of Edmund's henchman. When Albany enters with Goneril and Regan, the play is clearly far from over. Although Albany's speech to Edmund ("Sir, you have showed to-day your valiant strain . . ." V.iii.40−45) starts out in the standard fashion of victorious generals putting final touches to plays, Albany immediately turns his attention to the object of ours: he demands that Edmund turn Lear and Cordelia over to him. Edmund's smooth answer increases our fears for them; Edmund urged speed on the assassin, and now he says, "they are ready / To-morrow, or at further space, t'appear / Where you shall hold your session" (52–54). We fear that Albany may be diverted from his purpose; we have no reason to suspect that we will ourselves forget about the greatest unfinished business of the play. Albany is indeed diverted. He is not taken in by Edmund, but he does forget Cordelia and Lear to challenge Edmund's presumption. Thereupon the play and our attention imperceptibly skew toward the superimposed love-triangles (Edmund/Goneril/ Regan; Edmund/Goneril/Albany):

> *Albany.*   Sir, by your patience,
>   I hold you but a subject of this war,
>   Not as a brother.
> *Regan.*   That's as we list to grace him.
> . . . .
> *Goneril.*   Not so hot!
>
> [59-61, 66]

The focus of our attention now is Edmund. And we are smoothly led into the ceremonial conclusion Edgar has arranged and for which he has carefully prepared us: Edgar's trial-by-combat against Edmund. Edgar's victory—the triumph of virtue—has the feel of dramatic conclusion, and the lines that follow it offer an anthology of familiar signals that a play is ending: Edmund confesses and emphasizes the finality of his situation: "What you have charged me with, that have I done, / And more, much more. The time will bring it out. / 'Tis past, and so am I" (163–65). Edgar reveals himself (170), and passes a hollow but summary-sounding moral:

> The gods are just, and of our pleasant vices
> Make instruments to plague us.
> The dark and vicious place where thee he got
> Cost him his eyes.
>
> [171–74]

The easy readiness of Edmund's agreement ("Th' hast spoken right; 'tis true"—174) combines with the brothers' exchange of charity (166–67) to give their dialogue a quality comparable to the resolution at the end of a piece of music. Edmund then makes an almost explicit announcement that the dramatic entity is complete: "The wheel is come full circle; I am here" (175). Albany sounds like any one of dozens of rejoicing personages tying off the ends of a play by inviting narration of the events leading up to the hero's epiphany:

> *Albany.* Methought thy very gait did prophesy
>   A royal nobleness. I must embrace thee.
>   Let sorrow split my heart if ever I
>   Did hate thee, or thy father.
> *Edgar.*   Worthy prince, I know't.
> *Albany.* Where have you hid yourself?
>   How have you known the miseries of your father?
> *Edgar.* By nursing them, my lord. List a brief tale;
>   And when 'tis told, O that my heart would burst!
>
>   [176–83]

Edgar's account concludes with information new to us; he tells us once and for all what becomes of Gloucester:

> . . . some half hour past, when I was armed,
> Not sure, though hoping of this good success,
> I asked his blessing, and from first to last
> Told him our pilgrimage. But his flawed heart—
> Alack, too weak the conflict to support—
> 'Twixt two extremes of passion, joy and grief,
> Burst smilingly.
>
>   [194–200]

Edgar's narrative is obviously complete. But five lines later he continues—in a passage whose superfluity the Folio text can seem accidentally to vouch for by omitting it.[2] He begins on a line that summarizes my point, "This would have seemed a period":

> *Edgar.*   This would have seemed a period
>   To such as love not sorrow; but another,
>   To amplify too much, would make much more,
>   And top extremity.
>   Whilst I was big in clamor, came there in a man,
>   Who, having seen me in my worst estate,
>   Shunned my abhorred society; but then, finding
>   Who 'twas that so endured, with his strong arms
>   He fastened on my neck, and bellowed out
>   As he'd burst heaven, threw him on my father,
>   Told the most piteous tale of Lear and him
>   That ever ear received; which in recounting

His grief grew puissant, and the strings of life
Began to crack. Twice then the trumpets sounded,
And there I left him tranced.
Albany.   But who was this?
Edgar.   Kent, sir, the banished Kent; who in disguise
Followed his enemy king and did him service
Improper for a slave.

[205—22]

This passage—in which Edgar begins with the events of "some half
hour past" and works back to the beginning of Kent's history—is a
chiasmic reprise of Edgar's chronological account of his own activities
in disguise (it even echoes the word *burst* and the idea of bursting,
which framed the earlier account). The passage winds up and ties off
Kent's story as the previous one had Gloucester's, and, although
Edgar never says that Kent is dead, the parallelism—particularly that
between the substance and placement of the assertion that
Gloucester's heart "Burst smilingly" (200) and the assertion that the
strings of Kent's life "Began to crack" (218)—*does* say so. The Kent
story is over.

Eight lines later, as the fates of Goneril and Regan are being reported, Edgar casually says, "Here comes Kent"; Kent enters, and a
finished chapter continues.

Kent's first sentence violently aborts the ceremony of theatrical
conclusion that began when Albany called the herald to supervise the
formal combat between Edgar and Edmund:

Kent.   I am come
To bid my king and master aye good night.
Is he not here?
Albany.   Great thing of us forgot!

[235—37]

Albany's ridiculously phrased (and thus disconcertingly comic) cry of
surprise is curiously appropriate to an improbable theatrical situation
in which the characters onstage have forgotten all about the focal
figures of the scene.

That we, the audience, could also have forgotten about Lear and
Cordelia seems even more improbable, but I think audiences do just
that. For the audience, the smooth ceremony of conclusion presumably collapses only moments before Kent ends it for the characters. As

Edgar was putting a precise period to Kent's history, a gentleman entered with a bloody knife:

> *Gentleman.* Help, help! O, help!
> *Edgar.*   What kind of help?
> *Albany.*   Speak, man.
> *Edgar.* What means this bloody knife?
> *Gentleman.*   'Tis hot, it smokes.
>   It came even from the heart of—O, she's dead
>
>   [22–25)

Edgar's questions are our questions and open our minds to a forgotten need for help (note that the gentleman, whose message is that Goneril and Regan are dead, has no practical use for the help he asks). The imperfection of the gentleman's response to Edgar's questioning invites an audience to supply "Cordelia" to complete the interrupted phrase "from the heart of." When the gentleman does explain his distress—and when the play ambles on to sum up the careers of Goneril and Regan—the audience, though of course relieved that its immediate fears for Cordelia have not been realized, is likely to remain upset about Lear and Cordelia—perhaps not only upset in its concern for two virtuous characters in danger, but also upset in being the only party to the play that *is* concerned. Some nebulous uneasiness for the audience may also result from a sense of having gathered itself mentally in preparation for leaving a theatre where a play has formally concluded while its substance is still in urgent progress.[3]

Even after the characters have remembered that the main business of the play is unfinished, the audience's travail continues. All the different plots and subplots have tumbled out on the stage at once, and the characters leap from focus to focus like the mad Lear of earlier scenes. The frustration of the audience—which alone can focus its attention on the one vital action to be taken—is scrupulously intensified by Shakespeare; his care is epitomized by the parenthetic plea for haste with which Edmund delays the syntactic completion of "quickly send to the castle":

> *Edmund.* I pant for life. Some good I mean to do,
>   Despite of mine own nature. Quickly send—
>   Be brief in it—to th' castle, for my writ
>   Is on the life of Lear and on Cordelia.
>   Nay, send in time.

Albany.   Run, run, O run!
Edgar. To who, my lord? Who has the office? Send
   Thy token of reprieve.
Edmund. Well thought on. Take my sword;
   Give it to the captain.
Edgar.   Haste thee for thy life.

                                          [*Exit Officer.*]
                                          [244−52]

A moment later: *Enter Lear, with Cordelia in his arms,* and the most terrifying five minutes in literature have begun for the audience.

I submit that audiences are not shocked by the fact of Cordelia's death but by its situation and that audiences grieve not for Cordelia's physical vulnerability, or for the physical vulnerability of humankind, but for their own—our own—mental vulnerability, a vulnerability made absolutely inescapable when the play pushes inexorably beyond its own identity, rolling across and crushing the very framework that enables its audience to endure the otherwise terrifying explosion of all manner of ordinarily indispensable mental contrivances for isolating, limiting, and comprehending. When Lear enters howling in the last moments of the play, Shakespeare has already presented an action that is serious, of undoubted magnitude, *and complete;* he thereupon continues that action beyond the limits of the one category that no audience can expect to see challenged: Shakespeare presents the culminating events of his *story* after his *play* is over.

2. Something More to Say

An audience's experience of *King Lear* persistently reflects its characters' experience of the events depicted in it. The play makes its audience suffer *as* audience; the fact that *King Lear* ends but does not stop is only the biggest of a succession of similar facts about the play. The parallel between tests of the audience's theatrical endurance and the trials of the characters is illustrated in the two limp little speeches that intervene between Edgar's account of his father's death and his postscript on Kent. The first is by Edmund, and its lifelessness evokes a sense of unwarranted continuation:

            This speech of yours hath moved me,
And shall perchance do good; but speak you on—

You look as you had something more to say.

[V.iii.200—02]

In the second speech Albany explicitly takes up the threat of "more":

If there be more, more woeful, hold it in,
For I am almost ready to dissolve,
Hearing of this.

[203—05]

Edmund's speech both is and promises a burdensome and superfluous appendage to the audience's immediate theatrical experience; Albany protests the threat of augmentation, but—of course—protests it in the dimension of the dramatized events rather than of the dramatization.

Almost from the beginning, both the characters and the audience of *King Lear* must cope with the fact that the idea of the ultimate is *only* an idea, a hope, a working convenience.

The first speeches of *King Lear* are full of comparatives ("had more affected the Duke of Albany," "no dearer in my account," "know you better," "darker purpose," "no less loving son"). Lear introduces the superlative ("which of you shall we say doth love us most") and triggers an inflation in language and in its aspirations. Goneril begins her answer with comparatives and progresses toward the absolute (I.i.55—61); Regan outdoes her ("she comes too short . . . I profess / Myself an enemy to all other joys"—72—73). Cordelia's "Nothing" is the ultimate among ultimates; it makes retreat to relativism futile:

Cordelia.   . . . I love your Majesty
     According to my bond, no more nor less.
Lear. How, how, Cordelia? Mend your speech a little . . .

[92—94]

On the other hand, the realm of the absolute is paradoxically wanting in substitutes for the relative but serviceable sureness (definition, limitation, finality) available in the comfortable confines of comparison. Cordelia can say nothing "to draw / A third more opulent" than her sisters, but she *does* say, "Nothing": she cannot literally "love and be silent"—any more than Lear's hyperbole ("I disclaim all my parental care," "we have no such daughter") can literally obliterate

Cordelia's daughterhood or remove her from the category "daughter" in his speeches. Moreover, Cordelia *does* attempt to measure her love for Lear. The terms of her speech are relative ("That lord whose hand must take my plight shall carry / Half my love with him" —101—02); the speech is, in fact, an overt rejection of absolutes ("Sure I shall never marry like my sisters, / To love my father all" —103—04). But the rejection is itself an absolute, an absolute that collapses when she assents to Lear's response, "But goes thy heart with this?" (105). *Heart* in Lear's question is potentially a precise synonym for *love* in Cordelia's "carry half my love with him," but *love* (affection) in Cordelia's phrase is not synonymous with *heart* in Lear's question (a question that means "But do you really mean what you have just said?"). Cordelia does and does not contradict herself; her absolute allegiance to relativism is final, definitive, absolute—but only relative to the contextually, and thus tenuously, determined meaning of words.

That was a very abstruse example, offered only to suggest the depth to which the impossibility of finality permeates the play. For a simpler but equally incidental example, consider IV.vii.61, the line in which Lear specifies his age with absolute and absolutely ineffectual precision: "Fourscore and upward, not an hour more nor less." However, to see that the characters constantly and vainly strive to establish the limits of things, we need look at nothing more recondite than Edgar's stoic platitudes in the first lines of IV.i and the revision he offers after the entrance of the newly mutilated Gloucester a moment later (note the comfortable, comparative-like assumption of limits inherent in Edgar's use of superlatives in, "The lamentable change is from the best; / The worst returns to laughter"; like several other confident assertions in *King Lear,* this one reflects the idea of the wheel of fortune,[4] and a wheel is, above all, finite):

> Yet better thus, and known to be contemned,
> Than still contemned and flattered. To be worst,
> The lowest and most dejected thing of fortune,
> Stands still in esperance, lives not in fear.
> The lamentable change is from the best;
> The worst returns to laughter. Welcome then,
> Thou unsubstantial air that I embrace:

The wretch that thou hast blown unto the worst
Owes nothing to thy blasts.
  Enter Gloucester and an Old Man.
       But who comes here?
My father, poorly led? . . .
. . . .
O gods! Who is't can say 'I am at the worst'?
I am worse than e'er I was.

            [1–10, 25–26]

Lear's confident reservation of a hundred knights exemplifies a fruitless quest for definition of another sort. His initial scheme and his later dream of retirement in a walled prison with Cordelia exemplify yet another. The play is full of such quests, and the lines I quote for other purposes will include all the evidence one could wish. I prefer to turn my attention to the audience's similar efforts and frustrations. Those, too, come in many sizes and shapes. Take, for example, the experience of listening to the speech in which Lear first mentions the hundred knights. First, he makes an apparently absolute donation of everything ("I do invest you . . ."), *then,* after he has nothing, he tacks on his provisos:

Peace, Kent!
Come not between the dragon and his wrath.
I loved her most, and thought to set my rest
On her kind nursery.—Hence and avoid my sight!—
So be my grave my peace as here I give
Her father's heart from her! Call France. Who stirs!
Call Burgundy. Cornwall and Albany,
With my two daughters' dowers digest the third;
Let pride, which she calls plainness, marry her.
I do invest you jointly with my power,
Preeminence, and all the large effects
That troop with majesty. Ourself, by monthly course,
With reservation of an hundred knights,
By you to be sustained, shall our abode
Make with you by due turn. Only we shall retain
The name, and all th' addition to a king. The sway,
Revenue, execution of the rest,
Beloved sons, be yours; which to confirm,
This coronet part between you.

            [I.i.121–39]

I have quoted the whole speech because it is also the first of the many instances where Lear leaps suddenly from one topic to another. The first four speeches of *King Lear* are an orderly, efficient, and symmetrical introduction to two distinct plot lines in the play; the two plots are never distinct again, and from the time of Kent's first effort to interrupt Lear, *no* two things are ever distinct again. The scenes in which Lear's mind pounces upon one and then another topic are only exaggerated manifestations of the audience's constant difficulty in knowing where one topic ends and another begins.

The problem of knowing where something ends is, of course, a variation on the problems of knowing *if* something ends and whether it will ever end. Not ending is a primary characteristic of *King Lear.* The last sixteen lines of the play provide a brief sample of the varieties of inconclusiveness in *Lear;* an audience's experience of them is emblematic of the experience of the whole:

Lear. . . . Look there, look there—
  He dies.
Edgar.   He faints. My lord, my lord—
Kent. Break, heart, I prithee break!
Edgar.   Look up, my lord.
Kent. Vex not his ghost. O, let him pass! He hates him
  That would upon the rack of this tough world
  Stretch him out longer.
Edgar.   He is gone indeed.
Kent. The wonder is he hath endured so long;
  He but usurped his life.
Albany. Bear them from hence. Our present business
  Is general woe.
    [*To Kent and Edgar*] Friends of my soul, you twain
  Rule in this realm, and the gored state sustain.
Kent. I have a journey, sir, shortly to go.
  My master calls me; I must not say no.
Edgar. The weight of this sad time we must obey,
  Speak what we feel, not what we ought to say.
  The oldest hath borne most; we that are young
  Shall never see so much, nor live so long.

The play began in doubt about who would rule; the three final speeches, a reprise of the division of the kingdom in I.i, leave us in new doubt about who will rule: Albany? Albany, Kent, and ᴱ ¹

Kent and Edgar? Albany and Edgar? Edgar? Other varieties of inconclusiveness are exemplified in Kent's "I have a journey, sir, shortly to go. / My master calls me; I must not say no." It makes literally endless the endless succession of inconclusive journeys in *King Lear;* it echoes Kent's banishment in I.i and that of Cordelia, who said no. It also echoes and seems to repeat the substance of the sentence on which Kent entered this last scene, but—where "I am come / To bid my king and master aye good night" (235-36) said "I come to bid farewell to King Lear, my master, before I die"—this speech, where "master" fits both Lear and God,[5] conflates the separated, finite world and the infinite one referred to in the earlier speech; as a result, the promise of an afterlife acts upon the audience not to put a comfortable footnote to the lives we see ending but to extend our uncertainty into infinity.

These final speeches are also theatrically inconclusive. After the last speech, the Folios provide an urgently necessary stage direction, *Exeunt with a dead march.* This is the only one of the tragedies where the last lines do not point to an immediate offstage destination and invite the remaining characters to repair to it. The last lines of *King Lear* leave the survivors just to walk off the stage.

But my principal reason for focusing on these last sixteen lines is their substance. They dwell on the extreme *length* of Lear's suffering, and, in "shall never see so much," the last sentence comes close to pointing out the audience's parallel ordeal: *King Lear* is too long, almost unendurably so.

That sounds like an adverse criticism and ordinarily would be, but it is not so here, where I am arguing that the greatness of *Lear* derives from the confrontation it makes with inconclusiveness—arguing that the greatness of *King Lear* (in the metaphoric sense of "greatness") derives, at least in part, from its greatness (in the literal sense of "greatness"), its physical extent, its great duration. *King Lear* is not the longest of Shakespeare's plays, but—in ways comparable to those by which he makes Polonius, who does not speak much, seem always to be talking, and makes the verbose Coriolanus seem tight lipped—Shakespeare uses great and demonstrable technical skill to stretch his audience out upon the rack of this tough play.

The way of our escape and Lear's are one. We *want* Lear to die, just as, almost from the beginning, we have wanted the play to end. That does not mean that we are unfeeling toward Lear or that we dislike the play: watching *Lear* is not unlike waiting for the death of a dying friend; our eagerness for the end makes the friend no less dear. In his first speech Lear promises to die: he will, he says, "Unburdened crawl toward death" (I.i.41); for the progress of the play, *crawl* becomes the operative word. Even while the plot still offers, indeed promises, the happy ending the story has in all tellings previous to Shakespeare's, Lear's death is our only way out of a play that has been ready to end since it began. By its kind, the story of Lear and his three daughters promises a happy ending in which the virtuous youngest child proves herself so and the parent sees his error; but the play refuses to fulfill the generic promise inherent in its story.

After scene i the story of Lear and his daughters lacks only three quick steps to its conclusion: Goneril will show her colors; Regan will show hers; Cordelia will prove true.[6] Scene ii delays the predictable advance by opening up an echoing situation in Gloucester's family. In scene iii we see Goneril obviously preparing to do her duty by literary genre; in scene iv she does it. Lear now sees her as we see her, curses her, says "Away, away!" and exits (I.iv.280). Goneril has played out her part, and Lear is done with her. Four lines later Lear comes back onstage: "What, fifty of my followers at a clap? / Within a fort-night?" Both the reentrance and the new indignity Lear suffers are *extra;* the fact that Lear discovers the new and unexpected wrong offstage and discovers it to us only obliquely heightens our sense that the five-line resumption of his curse on Goneril (290−95) is excessive. It is theatrically excessive. We cannot pause to reason its need, and we do not grumble like Polonius listening to the player, but—as Lear curses on, doing again what was over and done with—we endure the slow passage of time like criminals in the stocks. When King Lear, the character, says "I'll resume the shape which thou dost think / I have cast off for ever" (I.iv.300−01), his hollow threat echoes the action of *King Lear,* a play that persists in resuming completed incidents and relapsing into past circumstances. In terms of our real experience, the experience of watching a play, we are, like Lear, oppressed beyond reasonable limits, even though the oppression is scaled to a three-hour stay at the theatre.

It takes Shakespeare about twenty minutes to get us to Regan and the next necessary step; but, when it does come, it is, appropriately, an intensified repetition of Lear's confrontation with the elder wicked sister. In II.iv.84—115, we are presented with an echo of Goneril's feigned sickness (I.iv.49) and with a variation on Oswald's negligence and refusal to come when Lear calls for him (I.iv.43—54, 75—79). Then, when Regan is on the point of teleological fulfillment, *Enter Goneril* (II.iv.184)—and we take a half-step back in our progress toward Cordelia, just when we seemed about to complete a step forward.

Similarly, Lear's meeting with Cordelia—which does not occur until IV.vii—is systematically delayed from IV.iii onward. (One reason, perhaps a main reason, why the meeting of Lear and Gloucester in IV.vi is so moving is that it is narratively superfluous).

A complete index of phenomena that avoid available means of concluding would note that Edgar and Kent continue to masquerade well after need has passed, and would include the curious fact that Lear's madness remains an impending event of the near future long after we have concluded that he is mad; but exhaustive demonstration is probably unnecessary. I will, however, discuss the part of *King Lear* that perennially prompts critics to talk about endurance: Lear's night on the heath.

Forty-five lines into III.ii, Lear's first scene in the storm, Kent says this:

> Since I was man,
> Such sheets of fire, such bursts of horrid thunder,
> Such groans of roaring wind and rain, I never
> Remember to have heard. Man's nature cannot carry
> Th' affliction nor the fear.
>
> [45—49]

No audience that has both heard Lear described in III.i as "contending with the fretful elements" and seen him do so at the beginning of this scene needs Kent's iterative and iteratively structured testimony to the horrors of the night and of Lear's situation. I think the power of the storm scenes derive not from the events portrayed but from contemplation of those events in combination with a real trial of our own endurance. Lear's agony and the audience's are totally different both in scale and kind, but they have the same remedy: Lear must "come out o' th' storm" (II.iv.304), must enter the hovel.

In his next speech after evaluating the storm, Kent tells us about the hovel (and does so in a scene that has so far been crowded with language of shelter, coverings, and roofs):

> Gracious my lord, hard by here is a hovel;
> Some friendship will it lend you 'against the tempest.
> Repose you there . . .
>
> [61−63]

Lear agrees immediately and with an unusual constancy of general focus:

> My wits begin to turn.
> Come on, my boy. How dost, my boy? Art cold?
> I am cold myself. Where is this straw, my fellow?
> The art of our necessities is strange,
> And can make vile things precious. Come, your hovel.
> Poor fool and knave, I have one part in my heart
> That's sorry yet for thee.
>
> [67−73]

The Fool sings a song; Lear says, "True, boy. Come bring us to this hovel" (78), exits with Kent, and—once the Fool concludes the seventeen-line prophecy with which he lengthens the scene—III.ii is over.

The next time we see Lear, Kent, and the Fool is in III.iv; they are still outdoors. The scene begins thus:

> *Enter Lear, Kent, and Fool.*
> Kent. Here is the place, my lord. Good my lord, enter.
>   The tyranny of the open night's too rough
>   For nature to endure.
>   *Storm still.*
> Lear.   Let me alone.
> Kent. Good my lord, enter here.
> Lear.   Wilt break my heart?
> Kent. I had rather break mine own. Good my lord, enter.
>
> [III.iv. 1−5]

Lear continues to rage, echoing the manner he abandoned when he agreed to seek the hovel and stressing his need of shelter ("In such a night / To shut me out! Pour on; I will endure"—17−18). Kent again urges Lear to enter the hovel—exit the stage and thereby end the scene. Kent gets Lear's attention. Lear says he will not go in; then says he will; then sends the Fool in "In, boy; go first"—26) and resumes his address to the whirlwind. One character, the Fool, has at last achieved shelter, but that achievement is counterproductive; the stage does not begin to empty but to fill. The Fool discovers Poor Tom; both come out into the storm; Gloucester arrives to second Kent's urging; Lear continues to delay ("First let me talk with this philosopher"—145). Finally—175 lines from Kent's "Here is the place" and a quarter-hour after a hovel hard by was offered to the expectations of the audience—Lear goes in.[7]

James Thurber's account of the Get-Ready Man is a fitting epigraph for an essay on *King Lear:* the Get-Ready Man was on the right track, but his prediction was really only wishful thinking—wishful thinking raised to assertion by a confidence in limits that can be maintained only by fanatics. Every time *King Lear* is performed, the theatre knows moments far more disquieting than the ones the Get-Ready Man shaped for the cultural elite of Columbus, Ohio.

3. *Identity and Definition*

What we ask of art is similar to what Lear asks of life: we ask that art have sure identity, which is to say, distinct, self-assertive limits. The greatness of Shakespeare derives, I believe, from his special use of literary tools that focus, isolate, and limit. He uses them so abundantly, and therefore so intensely, that they weigh sufficiently upon our consciousness to balance correspondingly intense counterforces, forces that repeatedly and insistently acknowledge: (1) that anything "cool reason ever comprehends" has "local habitation and a name" —exists in comprehensible form—*only* as it is arbitrarily isolated from the mass of experience; and (2) that in the blink of even a fanatic's eye it can and will rejoin that mass. A literary artist's means for defining his materials, fixing them in a relationship with one another and isolating them from other relationships, are of two, often overlapping, kinds: external—physical, chronological, and ideational boundaries; and internal—patterns of echoing situations, actions, ideas, words, and sounds that intensify the pertinence of the component parts to one another.

In *King Lear,* which gives up or disables all its external means of definition except the story line (and, in effect, gives that up too), the internally unifying devices of repetition are more material and more efficient than usual. For instance, the unifying effect of the two perceptibly distinct intertwined plots far outweighs the disunifying effect and is far greater than that of similarly echoing plots in plays where external boundaries operate conventionally. That is true even though the characters constantly undermine our sense of the likeness between the two family situations (and question the validity of the intellectual grasp derived from perceiving the likeness) by overstating and misreading the parallelism ("Gloucester's bastard son / Was kinder to his father than my daughters / Got 'tween the lawful sheets"—IV.vi.113—15).

I said earlier that the experience of the last sixteen lines of *King Lear* is emblematic of the experience of the whole. So is our experience of numerous other incidents, speeches, and smaller phenomena of the play. Paradoxically, the effect of this multiplicity is to contradict (and thus to counter, to balance, and to offset) the very quality that is duplicated: repeated evocation of a sense of indefiniteness generates a sense of pattern and thus of the wholeness, the identity, of the play. Similarly, as the play systematically destroys the intellectual comfort available from faith in kinds, it uses our perception of kind— shows us characters, events, speeches, and ideas that resemble one another—to compensate artistically for the intellectual terror that the same phenomena generate by illustrating the impossibility of definition.

For example, the play both contains and is contained by a vast network of overlapping and disparate likenesses among characters. Each major character is pointedly similar in some respect to several other characters to whom in some other respect he contrasts. Edgar, to take just one, echoes qualities of Cordelia (they are innocents wronged by their fathers); of Kent (each demeans, disguises, and endangers himself to serve his wronger); of Edmund (they are brothers with nearly interchangeable names, Edmund imitates a Bedlam beggar [I.ii.131—33] several scenes before Edgar does, and—for very different ends—both brothers practice upon their father's gullibility); of Gloucester (they are Edmund's victims, and he overtly equates them as foolishly credulous); of Goneril and Regan (they are elder children, who by the various rules of primogeniture are entitled to more than their siblings are, and who by the laws of fairy tales are entitled to less); of the Fool (both pretend simple-mindedness, and both follow a great man in decline); of Lear (Lear and Poor Tom are wandering, naked madmen); of Oswald (Poor Tom says that he was formerly "a servingman, proud in heart and mind; that . . . served the lust of [his] mistress' heart" [III.iv.81−83]); and of Albany (both evoke contempt from wicked characters who sneer at their virtuous ineffectuality).

Similarly, minor characters often gratuitously remind us of major ones whom they do not generally resemble; for instance, when Edmund's hired hangman says, "I cannot draw a cart, nor eat dried oats— / If it be man's work, I'll do't" (V.iii.38−39), he echoes lines spoken earlier by Kent (I.iv.10−34), by the Fool (II.iv.120−21), and by Edgar (III.iv.121−31). One cannot make sense of such correspondences, but one *feels* sense and order behind them.

The intensity of patterning in *King Lear* compensates for the equal intensity of its demonstration that the characters', the audience's, and all human perception of pattern is folly: the omnipresent, never-quite-circumscribable patterns testify—as faith in a religious metaphysic might—that a governing idea for the play, a lodestone for our values, exists just beyond our mental reach, that the play is faithful to it, and that our responses would prove similarly faithful and consistent if only we could interpret the oracular truths we feel but cannot see. That would explain our all-but-desperate need to believe that Lear learns something between Act I and his death, and the solemn vigor with which critics will fix on (and demand that the play be midwife to) a single pregnant phrase like "Ripeness is all"—even though it is manifest that in *King Lear* ripeness is next to nothing. ("Ripeness is all" has been the most popular of all candidates for the office of one-line kernel at the core of *King Lear;* if one must nominate a line, I suggest Gloucester's final one, his response to "Ripeness is all": "And that's true too"—V.ii.11).[8]

The ways in which pattern coexists with and compensates for inconclusiveness are well demonstrated at the most inconclusive point in the play. Shakespeare balances our sense that the "great thing of us forgot" is a structurally extraneous continuation of a completed action in two different ways. He fills the last minutes of the play with echoes that reach back and attach themselves to the body of the play (for

instance, Lear's efforts to coax life from Cordelia echo Cordelia's
ministrations to him in IV.vii; and Cordelia's death is both urgently
extraneous and the echo and fulfillment of the suggestion we heard
moments earlier when the gentleman said that the bloody knife "came
even from the heart of—O, she's dead"). More importantly, the
internal patterning of the lines between Lear's entrance with Cordelia
in his arms and the end of the play gives them an identity so insistent
that their inevitability is no more easily denied than our obvious need
to know what happens to Lear and Cordelia.

The last seventy lines cohere so tightly that any illustratively designed division must falsify their effect. I want to concentrate on the
largest of the patterns, what might be called a "now-dead, now-alive"
pattern; it is established in Lear's first speech over Cordelia and last
repeated (in reverse order) at Lear's own death, when Edgar first
thinks Lear has fainted and then realizes he is dead. Its first statement, however, includes a subpattern—a pair of three-speech frag-
ments, ineffectual interruptions of Lear's agony, first a line and a half
shared by Kent, Edgar, and Albany, then a line and a half shared by
Kent, Lear, and Edgar:

> *Lear.* Howl, howl, howl! O, you are men of stones.
>   Had I your tongues and eyes, I'ld use them so
>   That heaven's vault should crack. She's gone for ever.
>   I know when one is dead, and when one lives.
>   She's dead as earth. Lend me a looking glass.
>   If that her breath will mist or stain the stone,
>   Why then she lives.
> *Kent.*   Is this the promised end?
> *Edgar.* Or image of that horror?
> *Albany.*   Fall and cease.
> *Lear.* This feather stirs; she lives! If it be so,
>   It is a chance which does redeem all sorrows
>   That ever I have felt.
> *Kent.*   O my good master.
> *Lear.* Prithee away.
> *Edgar.*   'Tis noble Kent, your friend.
>
>   [V.iii.258−69]

The first speech in the foregoing quotation also presents an incidental
pattern in "you are men of stones" in the first lines and "stone," used

as a synonym for "looking glass" at the end of the speech—a pattern that offers one more instance of casual likeness between disparate things. Moreover, in addition to the ideationally insignificant verbal link between the two uses of the word *stone,* the two unrelated uses of the word sustain the larger pattern of violent alternation between evidence of certain lifelessness and evidence of life: in "you are men of stones" (a conflation of the synonymous assertions "you are men of stone" and "you are stones"), *stone* is emblematic of lifelessness; on the other hand, the same word describes the looking glass on which Lear hopes to register signs of life.[9]

The larger pattern, the one evoked in alternating conviction that Cordelia is dead and hope that she is alive, recurs in Lear's next speech:

> A plague upon you murderers, traitors all;
> I might have saved her; now she's gone for ever.
> Cordelia, Cordelia, stay a little. Ha,
> What is't thou say'st? Her voice was ever soft,
> Gentle, and low—an excellent thing in woman.
> I killed the slave that was a-hanging thee.
>
> [270—75]

The first line and a half echo the accusation and the conditional mood of the opening of the preceding passage, and "she's gone for ever" in line 271 is a simple repetition of the same words in line 260. In the earlier speech Lear had proposed a test for signs of life in Cordelia ("If that her breath will mist or stain the stone, / Why then she lives") and then read the results of an improvised test on a related principle ("This feather stirs; she lives"). Now, again on the basis of what passes Cordelia's lips, he listens for and thinks he hears her voice. As the tests echo one another, they also echo the test at the beginning of the play, the test in which Cordelia could not heave her heart into her mouth (I.i.91—92). As he did in the first scene of the play, Lear strains to hear Cordelia speak and hears nothing.

The next thirty lines are densely patterned. The pattern in which Lear is certain that Cordelia is dead and then just as certain that she lives is echoed in reversed order in his response to the question about the whereabouts of Kent's alter ego, Caius ("He's a good fellow, I can tell you that. / He'll strike, and quickly too. He's dead and rotten") and then extended when Kent says, "No, my good lord; I am the very man":

>   . . . I killed the slave that was a-hanging thee.
> *Gentleman.* 'Tis true, my lords, he did.
> *Lear.*   Did I not, fellow?
>   I have seen the day, with my good biting falchion
>   I would have made them skip. I am old now,
>   And these same crosses spoil me. Who are you?
>   Mine eyes are not o' the' best, I'll tell you straight.
> *Kent.* If Fortune brag of two she loved and hated,
>   One of them we behold.
> *Lear.* This is a dull sight. Are you not Kent?
> *Kent.*   The same:
>   Your servant Kent; where is your servant Caius?
> *Lear.* He's a good fellow, I can tell you that.
>   He'll strike, and quickly too. He's dead and rotten.
> *Kent.* No, my good lord; I am the very man.
> *Lear.* I'll see that straight.
> *Kent.* That from your first of difference and decay
>   Have followed your sad steps.
> *Lear.*   You are welcome hither.
> *Kent.* Nor no man else. All's cheerless, dark, and deadly.
>   Your eldest daughters have fordone themselves,
>   And desperately are dead.
> *Lear.*   Ay, so I think.
> *Albany.* He knows not what he says; and vain is it
>   That we present us to him.
> *Edgar.*   Very bootless.
>   *Enter a Messenger*
> *Messenger.* Edmund is dead, my lord.
> *Albany.*   That's but a trifle here.
>   You lords and noble friends, know our intent.
>   What comfort to this great decay may come
>   Shall be applied. For us, we will resign,
>   During the life of this old Majesty,
>   To him our absolute power; [*to Edgar and Kent*] you to
>   your rights,
>   With boot and such addition as your honors
>   Have more than merited. All friends shall taste

The wages of their virtue, and all foes
The cup of their deservings.—O, see, see!

[275–305]

These lines offer additional mental comfort in minor patterns. For instance, in the last speech of the thirty-line passage, Albany—again in response to a development in the Gloucester plot—sets out again to speak the last lines of a tragedy, and—in a situational echo of the earlier effort he made to finish the play, when, a hundred and twenty lines back, Edgar revealed himself and Lear and Cordelia were still unaccounted for—his effort to speak "what we ought to say" proves to be just what he says Edmund's death is: "but a trifle here." In "*King Lear:* The Final Lines," an essay that has not had the attention it deserves, John Shaw writes eloquently about Albany's speech:

> This speech of Albany's, beginning 'You lords and noble friends', has all the characteristics of a ceremonial closing address. It follows upon the news of the death of Edmund, the final *necessary* event of the tragedy, and one which might be expected to wind it all up . . . . Following the strict pattern of the other endings of tragedies, this speech, proclaimed by the man in authority, Albany, consciously re-established formal order. Lear will be restored. The good will be rewarded, the offenders punished, just as the Duke, for example, announces at the conclusion of *Romeo and Juliet:* 'Some shall be pardoned, and some punished'. . . . But the cadence with which Albany is trying to end the tragic events of *King Lear* turns out to be false, or, more accurately, 'interrupted'. . . . And we might imagine Albany uttering this speech—saying 'what we ought to say' . . . as if the tragedy were drawing to its close. For the speech is, after all, a formal declaration:
>
> You lords and noble friends, know our intent!
>
> With its usual formula of just distribution of reward and punishment, the speech apparently is moving toward its clinching couplet:
>
> > All friends shall taste
> > The wages of their virtue, and all foes
> > The cup of their deservings [bitter woes].
>
> We may well imagine both Albany's and the audience's shock, then, to behold a sudden change passing over the features of Lear, so that Albany must break off just at the expected couplet:
>
> > The cup of their deservings . . . O see, see![10]

In a sentence I omitted from the foregoing excerpt, Shaw remarks on Albany's persistence "in hoping to bring some 'comfort' to 'this great decay' by restoring . . . 'absolute power' " to Lear. "Nothing," Shaw justly says, "could be farther from the point" (p. 264). The ultimately petty social and political comforts in which Albany has faith are indeed irrelevant— but only to the situation dramatized. The speech and its interruption by considerations that dwarf it are, I think, to the point in that they offer quiet, unobserved comfort to an audience. They—as opposed to the substance they purvey—vouch for an orderliness in the play *as* play that persists even in defeat. The comfort I refer to is, surprisingly enough, of the kind formally inherent in the Book of Job, where—even as the sequence of events is devastating human belief in a morally ordered universe and, indeed, belief that there is any humanly comprehensible order to the universe—the narrative *is* orderly and thus a comfort. The rhymelike repetitions of "and I only am escaped alone to tell thee" that conclude each tale of woe make the experience of reading the Book of Job an exception to the rule the narrative exemplifies, the rule that there is no humanly perceptible rule by which the world works. There is similar comfort in the orderly process by which the orderly succession of Job's discomfortable comforters effectively exhaust the range of possible variations on "comfort that does not comfort."

The reason for my surprise at the likeness between the intellectual comfort provided by pattern in the Book of Job and the similar comfort that derives to an audience from the mere repetition of Albany's efforts to end *King Lear* is, of course, that in *Lear* regularity collapses not only in Lear's world—the fictional world in which, since it so resembles the real world, we are asked to see reality—but in the audience's own immediate world—the "world" the audience is familiar with from its previous theatrical experience. The glory of *King Lear* as an experience for its audience is in the fact that the play presents its morally capricious universe in a play that, paradoxically, is formally capricious and *also* uses pattern to do exactly what pattern usually does: assert the presence of an encompassing order in the *work* (as opposed to the world it describes). Albany's restitution speech and the inadequacy it acknowledges when Albany breaks off and says, "O, see, see!" embody the paradox precisely: both in substance and kind Albany's speech proclaims a return to order and gratifies one's assumptions that the norms of society and the norms of plays can be counted on; both Albany and his speech fail of their promised ends, and yet the mere repetition of the two kinds of failure balances and qualifies the effect of one of them, the failure of form.

The thirty-line passage that ends with Albany's speech also offers the comfort of lesser and simpler patterns. For example, consider the repetitions of *straight* and *boot;* the concentration of words related to seeing; and the sentence "Your eldest daughters have fordone themselves, / And desperately are dead"—the report of a fact which echoes both the substance and language of the fraud reported immediately before Lear's entrance, when Edmund revealed a plot to hang Cordelia and "lay the blame upon her own despair / That she fordid herself" (255—56).

But the same thirty lines take our minds across a crazy quilt of frames of reference—all pertinent, all reasonable, none deniable. From the time of his first defeat by Goneril, we have heard Lear slip from the contexts of particular topics of discussion into the pervasive context of his relation to his children. Here, in the oppressive presence of Cordelia's dead body, we are as Lear has been; we share Lear's inability to focus on revelations of identity and reports on the outcome of various plot lines ("That's but a trifle here").[11]

In addition, Shakespeare constructs dialogue that detaches from one pertinent evaluation system (or from an ostensible topic) and drifts into others. For example, when Lear says he killed the slave that was hanging Cordelia, we have just heard several minutes of evidence that he does not know what is real and what is imaginary. Kent and Edgar have refused to participate in Lear's moments of hope, and we have concluded that Lear is right when he says "She's gone forever" and wrong when he says "she lives." If the incidental gentleman did not bear instant witness to its truth, we would be inclined to put the claim to have killed the hangman with Lear's other fantasies. Earlier in the same speech Lear has said, "I might have saved her" (which implies not only that he did not save her but that, in effect at least, he was powerless against Edmund's henchman). Now we know for a fact that Lear killed the henchman while he was hanging Cordelia (which should imply that Cordelia was saved, and is certain evidence that Lear was not powerless). What we have here is a single action, two facts (Cordelia is dead, and the hangman is dead), and two related implications of the action, of which one accords with the facts and the other does not: although Lear is still a formidable swordsman and succeeded in his attack on the hangman, he failed in the purpose for which he attacked.

When Lear responds to the gentleman's testimony, he complicates the matter to a point where it becomes almost literally unthinkable:

> Did I not, fellow?
> I have seen the day, with my good biting falchion
> I would have made them skip. I am old now,
> And these same crosses spoil me.

These lines pertain to Lear's general condition but not to the specifics that evoke them. The speech begins in pride of this day's accomplishment as a swordsman, but it goes on, still pridefully, to boast of his past prowess in a way appropriate to a man frustrated by his impotence in combat and not by the larger impotence revealed in his failure to save Cordelia and in his incapacity to comprehend his situation.[12] As we listen to these speeches our mental state is as Lear's is and has been since his favorite daughter pleased him least and his less-loved daughters pleased him most, and since he ceased to rule and remained a king: what makes sense to us in one respect does not make sense in another.

The problem of Lear's success and failure against the hangman (which, by the way, presents a muted echo of, and participates in, the pattern made by Lear's vacillating certainty about Cordelia's death), is never resolved or even acknowledged. Lear's mind, after all, is gone. As earlier events moved forward before Lear could unravel their causes and effects, so this speech (where Lear himself is the inevitable force powered by multiple logics and we are the hopeless comprehenders), moves on inexorably, abruptly abandoning one line of thought and —in the moment of violent discontinuity—picking up others. Lear says, "Who are you?" and the dialogue proceeds toward his recognition of Kent and a discussion of the identity and present condition of Caius. When Lear abandons the topic of his swordsmanship, his sudden shift of topic recalls a pattern of mad behavior to which we became accustomed as we watched his progress from Goneril's house to Gloucester's to the heath to Dover. We are reminded that we are listening to a madman, and the reminder is a particularized justification of Lear's protestations of disability. Moreover, Lear's new topic, Kent's identity, is a reassuring recurrence to Kent's ignored self-revelation of a few moments before:

> Who are you?
> Mine eyes are not o' th' best, I'll tell you straight.
> *Kent.* If Fortune brag of two she loved and hated,
> One of them we behold.
> *Lear.* This is a dull sight. Are you not Kent?

On the other hand, Kent's lines on Fortune throw our minds into yet another situation where assertions adhere to more than one logic. Kent's comment, while effectively clear enough in substance, is roundabout in a way that puts a listener through a miniature maze from which the listener emerges only by shrugging the comment off as rhetorical fancywork. When we hear of two that Fortune loved and hated, we are looking at two such: Lear and Cordelia. It doesn't matter that we do not know why Kent specifies two, why he then limits our concern to one, or why he fails to specify which one; we cannot pause to worry; we just take the sentence as another comment on Lear's pitiful state. The sentence does, however, exercise its listener's consciousness in one more experience of perceiving an arbitrarily fixed object of concern which is then arbitrarily redefined in a way that undoes the whole action of definition.

As we watch and hear the play, it persists in veering violently from its course, but in doing so it offers straws for the understanding to sense or clutch at ("loved" and "hated," for instance, are *two,* and Lear and Cordelia appear here only as objects of *one* of Fortune's two specified emotions, her hatred). Moreover, since the play observes so many patterns of repetition, most discontinuities are also reassuring continuations of one or more patterns other than the one broken. Consider, for example, the next sequence of lines. Lear's "This is a dull sight" has no clear, fixed referent. Following immediately upon Kent's comment on what "we behold," "This" seems to mean the sight before us ("this is a melancholy sight to behold"), and since the principal object of our view and Lear's is Cordelia, "This" also suggests the corpse. On the other hand, although "This" is unlikely to say "mine" to an audience, "This is a dull sight" comes to suggest "My eyesight is dull"—a meaning evoked by the completed line

("This is a dull sight. Are you not Kent?") and seconded by the distant and syntactically improbable antecedent provided by "Mine eyes are not o' th' best, I'll tell you straight" (280) and its echo in "I'll see that straight" (288)—which continues the language of eyesight by using "see" to mean "understand" and conflates the sense of one sentence—"Mine eyes are not o' th' best"—from the earlier line and the structure and diction of the other—"I'll tell you straight." If, however, we may reasonably say that—having heard Lear talk about eyesight and having heard "Are you not Kent?"—an audience can understand "This is a dull sight" as a comment on Lear's difficulty in seeing through tears, it is just as reasonable to remember that this audience is used to Lear's sudden shifts of focus, and is prepared to hear the assertion about sight in ideational isolation from the question to Kent.

As Kent strives to reveal his history, Lear's mental dislocation becomes increasingly complete:

Lear. This is a dull sight. Are you not Kent?
Kent.   The same:
   Your servant Kent; where is your servant Caius?
Lear. He's a good fellow, I can tell you that.
   He'll strike, and quickly too. He's dead and rotten.
Kent. No, my good lord; I am the very man.
Lear. I'll see that straight.
Kent. That from your first of difference and decay
   Have followed your sad steps.
Lear.   You are welcome hither.
Kent. Nor no man else. All's cheerless, dark, and deadly.
   Your eldest daughters have fordone themselves,
   And desperately are dead.
Lear.   Ay, so I think.
Albany. He knows not what he says; and vain is it
   That we present us to him.
Edgar.   Very bootless.

[283—95]

Albany's and Edgar's comments sum up Lear's situation, but, as they work to pin down the cause of the discontinuity of the preceding dialogue, they account only for *a* cause. They confirm and objectify our conclusions about Lear's erratic answers; they ignore Kent's "Nor no man else"—a statement much less easy to comprehend comfortably. Like the lines I have just discussed, the reference of "Nor no man else" is unfixed and multiple; its effect may be infered from this brave editorial effort to explain it (by Kenneth Muir in his Arden edition [London, 1952, rev. ed., London and Cambridge, Mass., 1957]):

> This may mean: "No, neither I, nor any man, is welcome". Or it may mean: "And there was no one else followed you in the days of your misfortunes" (though the Fool was also there). But I think it probably refers back to "I am the very man" . . . and that it means simply "I am really him and no one else."

The proximity of "nor no man else" to Lear's welcome and to "All's cheerless, dark, and deadly" makes "Nor no man else" a vague and syntactically unattached comment on the general scene. Kent's perseverance across Lear's interjections makes this an inaccurate and still syntactically random continuation from "followed your sad steps." Muir decides in favor of the most distant referent, the only one with which "Nor no man else" fits syntactically, but even that solution adds a challenge to comprehension because we hear Kent say that he is Caius and no one else in the course of explaining that he has had two identities.

The last of Lear's statements of despair of Cordelia and hope for her, his inconclusive, unconcluded death speech, assaults our minds more violently than anything else in the play:

> And my poor fool is hanged: no, no, no life?
> Why should a dog, a horse, a rat, have life,
> And thou no breath at all? Thou'lt come no more,
> Never, never, never, never, never.
> Pray you undo this button, Thank you, sir.
> Do you see this? Look on her! Look her lips,
> Look there, look there—

[306—12]

"And my poor fool is hanged" explodes our confidence that we know what we perceive—just as Lear's death in apparent delusion explodes our hope that his travail will have made him illusion proof. Lear speaks the line over the body of Cordelia who has been hanged, but *fool* seems a strange choice of words. *Although* the word *fool* was regularly applied to innocent creatures as a term of pity and/or endear-

ment, *although* Shakespeare often uses the word to refer to children
and to animals ("fool" here is followed immediately by "a dog, a
horse, a rat"), *although* Shakespeare has played on the two senses of
fool earlier in this very play (I.iii. 19: "Old fools are babes again"), *and*
although that information suffices to explain all Renaissance uses of
fool where the meaning "innocent" is clear from context and a scholarly footnote functions primarily as a historical persuader against
student ingenuity, no footnote can dispel the impression that "my
poor fool" refers to Lear's Fool. The context that dictates that *fool* refer
to Cordelia—Lear's position over her body, the pronoun *thou,* her
death by hanging, and the echo of two earlier cycles of grief and
hope—coexists with the context provided by a play in which one
character is a fool, a professional clown, who has vanished noiselessly
during Act III, and by a scene punctuated with six reports of offstage
deaths.[13] Moreover, the syntactic habit of the word *and* is to introduce material relatively extraneous to what precedes it;[14] the word
appears in a play where such sudden unions of topic are habitual (see,
for instance, I.ii.23−26 and 111−14: Gloucester's entrance and exit
lines in scene ii) and is spoken by a character who has been erratically
springing from one mental fix to another for five acts. Here again,
one sentence, "And my poor fool is hanged," makes two distinct and
yet inseparable statements. Our minds are for a moment firmly fixed
in two places at once. Over and over again in this scene and throughout *King Lear,* an audience thinks in multiple dimensions—
entertains two or more precise understandings at once, understandings that might, but do not, clash in the mind. Such moments are to
the experiences of puns, malapropisms, and our mixed but separable
feelings about Hotspur, Prospero, Edmund, or Cordelia as the
strength of God is to the strength of Hamlet or Hercules.

4. Altogether Fool

The strange double reference of *fool* in Lear's last speech is the culmi-
nation of a kind of effect that the play achieves in many varieties and
from many materials.[15] Each variety and each instance is one in which
a mental boundary vanishes, fails, or is destroyed. An audience's
experience of the word *fool,* the Fool, and the idea of foolishness in
King Lear is like its experience of another pattern (with which, be-

cause "a natural" is a fool, it overlaps): the iterative pattern made up of the word *natural,* of its various senses and forms, and of their equally various synonyms and antonyms. Both experiences are comparable to the experience of the last moments of the play where, as I said in section 3, a sense of pattern (and hence of order, control, identity, limit) is—paradoxically—evoked by a sequence of elements that generate incidental uncertainty in us—a sequence that demonstrates that all categorization, limitation, definition is an arbitrary and unreliable mental convenience.

The well-documented instability of the diction in *King Lear* is obviously pertinent to my topic, but, by and large, I will take its inclusion in the roster of inefficient boundaries for obvious and for granted.[16] For example, the chameleon behavior of *natural, kind,* and words and ideas related to them has been much discussed and well discussed; I have nothing to add—except perhaps to point out that *genre* is a synonym of *nature* and of *kind* and to suggest that, in violating its own manifest nature, *King Lear* explores our trust in the idea of the natural and questions its validity in a dimension beyond—and, for an audience, experientially more immediate than —the fiction the play enacts. Discussions of references to eyesight have also fed the mills of criticism for several decades. Similar investigations of the recurring but troublesomely flexible word *fortune* (which means variously "luck," "accident," "good luck," "wealth," "fate," and the goddess Fortuna) could also have been a staple and may yet become one.[17]

As a target of critical attention, only *nature* has surpassed the word *fool* and ideas of foolishness in popularity. Only a natural fool of fortune would try to digest and regurgitate all the evidence or even assemble a full index of the guises of "fool." Nonetheless—since I have made a start with it—I will use "fool" as a convenient focus for further discussion of boundlessness in *Lear.* I will, however, concentrate on instabilities woven so deeply into the fabric of the play—and so subtly unsettling to our faith in limits—that attempts to point out and describe examples may be critical folly. I risk the charge of ingenuity not only because each of the following instances evokes a sense of limitless relationship and unlimited means of relating, but because each is itself so transitory. The phenomena I will describe subvert our comforting belief in irrelevancy by arousing our sense of the irrelevant—by making us aware of open avenues for thought which the play does not pause to acknowledge and which thus feel to us like momentary vagaries of our own minds. The attractive nuisance of ideational static tempts an audience's mind within inches of the extravagance which, for differing reasons and with differing effects, is a common denominator of Lear's thinking, the Fool's, and Edgar's as they leap from one frame of reference to another.

These lines occur just after Edgar's first appearance as Poor Tom:

Lear.   Nothing could have subdued nature
    To such a lowness but his unkind daughters.
    Is it the fashion that discarded fathers
    Should have thus little mercy on their flesh?
    Judicious punishment—'twas this flesh begot
    Those pelican daughters.
Edgar. Pillicock sat on Pillicock Hill. Alow, alow, loo, loo!
Fool. This cold night will turn us all to fools and madmen.
Edgar.   Take heed o' th' foul fiend; obey thy parents;
    keep thy words' justice; swear not; commit not with
    man's sworn spouse; set not thy sweet heart on proud
    array. Tom's acold.

                                        [III.iv.68−79]

The various and overlapping relationships that crosshatch these lines are established by methods that include—and are all of a kind with—those ordinarily pointed out to students of literature, but some of them extend poetic patterning principles beyond the boundaries of system. The speeches are pulled together by nonsignifying alliteration—simple ("fashion," "fathers," "flesh," "fools," "foul fiend") and complex ("a lowness," "Alow, alow" ["loo, loo," "fools," "foul"], "acold")—and by a phonetic equation ("pelican," "Pillicock") that impinges on our consciousness as a mad substitute for a logical one. The passage gets thematic coherence from the kinship among the topic of relations between parents and children, the nursery sound and diction of "Pillicock [equated with "darling" by Florio (1598) and "prettie knave" by Cotgrave (1611)] sat on Pillicock Hill," and Edgar's medley of snatches from the catechism. These rather straightforward coherences—which counteract the logical incoherence of the dialogue—coexist with others in which words and ideas are strung together by common denominators as abstruse and as wantonly variable as those that direct the conversation of Lear, Edgar, and the Fool. Puns, synonyms, repetitions, and paired contraries offer potential junctions from which the mind might follow irrelevant, logically random trains of thought. Like Lear's mind when it shifts from attaching the particulars of his own misery to the particulars of Tom's ("Is it the fashion that discarded fathers / Should have thus little mercy on their flesh?") through the summary comment, "judicious punishment," to attaching the particulars of Tom's misery to his own (" 'twas this flesh begot / Those pelican daughters"), our minds pass through a maze of doorways to madmen's logic and are repeatedly tempted to demonstrate our own susceptibility to abnormal thinking.

Take, for example, the fusion and confusion of agents in the speech that concludes with "pelican daughters": the potentially ambiguous diction of the second sentence makes it include both a suggestion of the wrongs done Cordelia and Edgar by their fathers and a shadowed paraphrase of the first sentence—a paraphrase that would be present in fact if the position of "discarded fathers" and "their flesh" were reversed ("their flesh [i.e., their own flesh and blood] . . . have little mercy on discarded fathers"), and which *is* present inferentially in the pelican allusion. The mythology of pelicans sums up the confusion of agency in the speech: some versions stress the sacrifice of the mother who pierces her own breast to feed her young; others stress the cruelty of the chicks and give the impression that the chicks pierce the mother's flesh to nurse on her blood (see Kenneth Muir's notes to the Arden *Lear*). In the passage as a whole, each of the following groups of words and phrases can be justified by some ideational or phonetic ordering system or combination of systems: "subdued," "lowness," "hill," and "proud"; "pelican" (= a bird), "-cock," and "Alow, alow, loo, loo" (= like a hunter's cry to his hawk); "pelican" (= bird, fowl), "fools," and "foul"; "begot," "Pillicock sat on Pillicock Hill,"[18] "commit not with man's sworn spouse," and "proud";[19] "sat" and "set"; "spouse" and "sweet heart"; "swear not" and "sweet heart"; "swear not" and "sworn spouse"; "keep thy words' justice" and "swear not"; "mercy" and "justice"; "Judicious punishment" and "Take heed o' th' foul fiend"; "fashion" and "proud array"; "on their flesh," "on Pillicock Hill," and "on proud array." I do not mean to suggest that these groups have ever been consciously perceived by an audience—any more than standard polyptoton ("Judicious," "justice"; "swear," "sworn") and conduplicatio (in *not*) are. Nor do I think that every one of them acts even minimally on every member of an audience. I do say, however, that the nature of this passage and of many, many others in *King Lear* is such as to excite the mental faculty by which we make puns and see ironies, by which frivolously or solemnly we leave one logic and slip into another, by which our arbitrarily focused minds suddenly recognize and acknowledge impertinent but undeniable other ways and realms of thought.

Throughout his career Shakespeare shows interest in words like *break, doubt, fellow, let, pitch, sense, stoop,* and *rest*—which have one meaning in one context and an opposite meaning in another—and with words like *dear* and *care*—which have good or bad connotations depending upon their contexts. The words *fool, nature,* and *fortune* provide a complex variation on this interest and the kind of mental exercise it leads to. Another variation, one that, like the tangled networks of coherence in the Pillicock passage, evokes a vague—and therefore particularly disturbing—sense of limitlessness, is provided by the use of *fool* and *knave* both as effective synonyms (I.iv.41, III.ii.72) and as effective antonyms (II.iv.73, 81). Similarly—in a play where we are under constant pressure to distinguish fools from madmen and to distinguish among the various kinds and degrees of real, supposed, or affected madness and foolishness—we also accept "fools and madmen" as if *fool* and *madman* were synonyms.

The word *fool* repeatedly fails—is insufficient to define the characters or the kinds of behavior to which it pertains and is inconsistent about the qualities it isolates. The whole issue is encapsulated when the Fool demonstrates the justice of Kent's "This is not altogether fool, my lord" by carefully misconstruing it to mean that the Fool has no monopoly on foolishness:

No, faith; lords and great men will not let me. If I
had a monopoly out, they would have part on't. And
ladies too, they will not let me have all the fool to
myself; they'll be snatching.

[I.iv.145–48]

Neither the dividing lines among the various categories labeled "fool" nor those between fools and madmen are easy to fix in *King Lear*.

Lear's foolishness in scene i is called madness by Kent; Lear later is insane; the Fool calls Lear a fool; and so on.

The whole subject of the fluidity of "fool" and "madman" is summed up in I.v, when Lear tries his hand at clowning; there ensues a fusion and confusion of overlapping categories of topic and meaning that at last trails off and departs for infinity when the Fool jumps from *mad*ness, a topic that emerged from a discussion of joke making, to a laughing *maid*.[20] These are the last lines of I.v (Lear, whom we will next see at *Gloucester's* castle, is preparing to depart for *Regan's* castle, which, apparently, is either called Gloucester or is at a place called Gloucester [I.v.1]):

> *Lear.* I will forget my nature. So kind a father!—
>   Be my horses ready?
> *Fool.* Thy asses are gone about 'em. The reason why the seven stars are
>   no moe than seven is a pretty reason.
> *Lear.* Because they are not eight.
> *Fool.* Yes indeed. Thou wouldst make a good fool.
> *Lear.* To take 't again perforce—Monster ingratitude!
> *Fool.* If thou wert my fool, nuncle, I'ld have thee beaten for being old
>   before thy time.
> *Lear.* How's that?
> *Fool.* Thou shouldst not have been old till thou hadst been wise.
> *Lear.* O, let me not be mad, not mad, sweet heaven!
>   Keep me in temper; I would not be mad!
>   [*Enter a Gentleman.*]
>   How now, are the horses ready?
> *Gentleman.* Ready, my lord.
> *Lear.* Come, boy.
> *Fool.* She that's a maid now, and laughs at my departure,
>   Shall not be a maid long, unless things be cut shorter.
>   *Exeunt.*
>   [I.v.28−46]

Lear is not alone in threatening to usurp the Fool's office as professional clown. When the disguised Kent auditions for Lear's retinue, he sounds like—and Lear treats him like—a professional jester:

> *Lear.* . . . How now, what art thou?
> *Kent.* A man, sir.
> *Lear.* What dost thou profess? What wouldst thou with us?

Kent. I do profess to be no less than I seem, to serve him truly that will
   put me in trust, to love him that is honest, to converse with him that
   is wise and says little, to fear judgment, to fight when I cannot
   choose, and to eat no fish.
Lear. What art thou?
Kent. A very honest-hearted fellow, and as poor as the King.
Lear. If thou be'st as poor for a subject as he's for a king, thou art poor
   enough. . . .
. . . .
Lear. What services canst thou do?
Kent. I can keep honest counsel, ride, run, mar a curious tale in telling
   it, and deliver a plain message bluntly. That which ordinary men are
   fit for I am qualified in, and the best of me is diligence.
Lear. How old art thou?
Kent. Not so young, sir, to love a woman for singing, nor so old to dote
   on her for anything. I have years on my back forty-eight.
Lear. Follow me; thou shalt serve me. If I like thee no worse after
   dinner, I will not part from thee yet. Dinner, ho, dinner! Where's
   my knave? my fool?

[I.iv.9—21, 30—41]

The Fool's first action in the play is a suggestion that Kent's
persona impinges on the office of fool: "Let me hire him too. Here's
my coxcomb" (I.iv.90). Similarly, Edgar, whose disguise as an idiot
beggar is an incursion upon the category "fool" in any case, is inter-
viewed by Lear, Kent, and Gloucester in exchanges (III.iv.80—95,
118—32) that echo the passage in which Kent's persona was established. Edgar immediately takes over the Fool's habit of breaking
into snatches of obscurely pregnant song, and Poor Tom's first
exit lines ("Child Rowland to the dark tower came . . ."—III.iv.
173—75), sound like and replace the similar set pieces with which the
Fool has closed earlier scenes.

The Fool himself breaks out of every category in which he might be
fixed and out of the play itself. When Kent says "This is not altogether fool," we understand that the Fool is no idiot and also that
he is no mere joke teller; this is a "wise fool," a *literal* "oxymoron"—a
type beloved in literature, a stock paradox with whom our minds are
comfortable. The Fool's first exit speech is typical of the traditional
character; it is a vatic bonbon in which the mode is clownish and
impertinent and the matter is wise and pertinent to Lear's situation:

Nuncle Lear, nuncle Lear, tarry. Take the fool with thee.
  A fox, when one has caught her,
  And such a daughter,
  Should sure to the slaughter,
  If my cap would buy a halter.
  So the fool follows after.

[I.iv. 306–12]

A real-life professional clown could have been expected to perform a
comic routine at his exit; so could a character who is a professional
clown. The Fool's double action—as comedian retained by King Lear
and comedian performing before a theatre audience—is here a single
action. However, where the Fool's first exit from the stage is indistinguishable from his exit from a room in Goneril's house, his next
("She that's a maid . . .") has no audience in the fiction; its substance participates in the thematic undercurrent of sexual wantonness
in the play, but it is addressed to, and concerns only, the playhouse
audience.

Clowns in plays commonly did, and often still do, depart from
their concerns as characters to fool with the audience. But we have
been led to assume that the Fool in *Lear* has abdicated the privilege of
ordinary theatrical clowns in order to join the ranks of Tiresias-like
fools extraordinary. In the scene concluded by the couplet on maids,
the Fool has alternated between showing us sample swatches of the
traditional comic material of court jesters and commenting wisely on
Lear's folly; he has been consistent to his type, wise fool, a type entirely defined by violations of our expectations about the behavior of
fools. When Lear's Fool suddenly talks to the audience like an ordinary fool in an ordinary play, the established paradox of the wise idiot
is both capped and deflated in a parallel action whereby the humble
seer turns momentarily and unexpectedly into an irresponsible, frivolous clown.

A similar sort of explosion occurs on a larger scale in III.ii, where
the Fool's exit lines are to theatrical nature as the storm is to the
natural world:

Fool. [*sings*]
  He that has and a little tiny wit,
      With, heigh-ho, the wind and the rain,

    Must make content with his fortunes fit
        Though the rain it raineth every day.
Lear. True, boy. Come, bring us to this hovel.

                                         Exit [*with Kent*].

Fool. This is a brave night to cool a courtesan.
    I'll speak a prophecy ere I go:
    When priests are more in word than matter;
    When brewers mar their malt with water;
    When nobles are their tailors' tutors,
    No heretics burned, but wenches' suitors;
    When every case in law is right,
    No squire in debt nor no poor knight;
    When slanders do not live in tongues,
    Nor cutpurses come not to throngs;
    When usurers tell their gold i' th' field,
    And bawds and whores do churches build—
    Then shall the realm of Albion
    Come to great confusion.
    Then comes the time, who lives to see't,
    That going shall be used with feet.
    This prophecy Merlin shall make, for I live before
    his time.   *Exit*
                                     [III.ii.74−96]

By delaying the conclusion of the scene, these speeches of the Fool participate in the systematic frustration of our desire to see Lear sheltered—and mirror it by being composed of several superfluous repetitions of a superfluity. The song before Lear's exit fulfills the function of an exit routine. "This is a brave night to cool a courtesan" fills it again. And so does the prophecy that follows. These last two also violate the dramatic illusion, as the previous exit speech had done. Here, however, the destruction of mental limits and categories extends to time and is more devastating. By definition, a prophecy concerns future time, but in this play all definition is illusory.

    Much ingenuity has been expended on the prophecy, but scholarly bridgework is inevitably insignificant and ineffective as compared with the qualities that prompt it—in this case qualities so disturbing that rational beings feel called upon to argue the prophecy away or to crush it a little and make it bow to reason. Our immediate response to the first two conditions in the prophecy is that they are not future but present evils: priests who profess more than they do and brewers who water their beer are chronic.

The next two lines are less clear and more disturbing. Just as we recognize the word *bureaucrat* in any modern sentence as a signal that we are expected to feel contempt, a Renaissance audience was conditioned to take *any* mention of dealings between gentlemen and their tailors as an invitation to moralistic disdain. Moreover, repetition of the *when* construction also suggests that the substance of line 3 is another current evil similar to those presented by the *when* construction of the first two lines. Line 3 could be read as a third item in the list of current abuses (nobles know, care, and fuss more about fashion than tailors do) or as a future good (the behavior, values, and opinions of nobles will not be dictated by their tailors); but as the line passes in the theatre an audience presumably only feels further disoriented and has no time to speculate on the reason. The fourth line is similar; it is hard to decide—and one has no time to wonder—whether the time when there are "No heretics burned, but wenches' suitors" is present or future, desirable or undesirable. Line 4 has a cadence-like finality because it breaks from the *when* pattern, but the Fool does not advance to the *then* of his prophecy. The next line makes a fresh start on a fresh *when*; then comes another *no* construction, another *when,* a *nor* construction, a *when . . . and,* and, at long last, *then.*

Not only does the prophecy duplicate the general pattern of the play by failing to come to a conclusion when it signals one, but our experience with the lines on law, debt, slanders, cutpurses, usurers, and whores are to our experience of the first four lines as our experience of the Fool's suddenly clownish exit speeches are to his apparently fixed character as wise fool. We have just learned that the *when*s of this particular prophecy do not refer to the future but mean "in as much as," "since"; now we get what we are newly weaned from demanding: "When every case in law is right" and five more conditions that are clearly future and apparently desirable. The *then* clause, when it does come, sounds just as prophecy should sound, but *then* has become meaningless. The *then* clause is no more final than anything else in the speech; it is followed by another, in which *then* is also meaningless, although its futurity is underscored, and in which the generic givens of prophecy are obliterated absolutely: we can imagine no time past, present, or future when walking will be done other than with feet.

Now, at last, the prophecy is finished. But the speech is not. We have endured the breaking of the category "fool," the category "wise fool," and the category "prophecy"; now we face the frailty of the category "play." The Fool speaks one more line before he goes, a line of flat prose in which he blows apart the chronological limits of the fiction and, indeed, all divisions between character and actor, character and audience, past and present, past and future, future and present: "This prophecy Merlin shall make, for I live before his time." As the speech went on, we tried gamely to get our bearings and hear sense in nonsense; now we arrive at a conclusion that implies that there are no bearings to get. As an audience of *King Lear,* we have cause to cry that we are come to this "stage of fools." We, who are upon the great stage, are, for the duration of the play at least, aware that any sense we have of our location is false.

5. Inconclusion

To make a work of art—to give local habitation and nameability to an airy nothing or a portion of physical substance—is to make an identity. I have argued that *King Lear* both is and is not an identity —that our sense that it inhabits only its own mental space is countered by a sense that it and those of its elements that I have discussed are unstable, turn into or fuse into other things. The identities of the characters and our evaluations of them belong in the catalogue of elements that duplicate the simultaneously fixed and unfixed quality of the whole of *King Lear.* By way of transition from discussing an audience's experience of words in *Lear* and in support of the thesis that all the phenomena I talk about are of one general kind (that to relate an audience's *conclusions* about characters and events to the foregoing discussions of *ends, limits,* and *terms* is to do more than play on words), I will begin by talking about the likeness and difference of Goneril and Regan, a likeness and difference played out both in the large action of the play and in the following short exchange on the subject:

> *Fool.* Shalt see thy other daughter will use thee kindly; for though she's
> as like this as a crab's like an apple, yet I can tell what I can tell.

Lear. What canst tell, boy?

Fool. She will taste as like this as a crab does to a crab. Thou canst tell why one's nose stands i' th' middle on's face?

Lear. No.

Fool. Why, to keep one's eyes of either side 's nose, that what a man cannot smell out he may spy into.

Lear. I did her wrong.

Fool. Canst tell how an oyster makes his shell?

Lear. No.

Fool. Nor I neither; but I can tell why a snail has a house.

Lear. Why?

Fool. Why, to put 's head in; not to give it away to his daughters, and leave his horns without a case.

Lear. I will forget my nature. So kind a father!

[I.v.12—28]

When the Fool says "Shalt see thy other daughter will use thee kindly," the tone and context of the line make "tenderly" the primary meaning of *kindly*. Our knowledge of Regan's likeness to Goneril and of the Fool's opinion of both sisters makes that sense most inappropriate. As the speech continues, it moves toward explaining that to say Regan will act "kindly" is to say that she will act according to her *own* nature. But the speech does not move there directly: "for though" suggests that the sentence is about to confront our objections to the idea that Regan will behave tenderly, benevolently, or humanely; "for though she's as like this as a crab" confirms that suggestion, and "crab" probably suggests that both sisters are crabbed, are like pinching crustaceans; "for though she's as like this as a crab's like an apple" thus strikes us as a statement that the sisters are unlike (crustaceans are unlike apples), that the sisters are alike (crab apples *are* apples), and again that the sisters are unlike (crab apples are so called because they are sour and one thinks of apples as sweet). When the Fool completes his "although . . . but" construction with "she will taste as like this as a crab does to a crab," we understand the whole sentence as an assertion of likeness, both because we know that Goneril and Regan are alike, and because the proposition x is like x is incontrovertible. On the other hand, both the construction ("thy other daughter will use thee kindly . . . though . . . yet . . .") and the previously established versatility of the word *crab* make the completed statement seem to confirm the original assertion that Regan will be benevolent—an assertion we cannot believe the Fool would make. Our miniature mental decathlon is thereupon prolonged by a last incidental mental hurdle: the Fool gives up the topic of crab apples only to take up oysters and snails.[21]

Something less complex but similar happens over our three-hour experience of the play. Shakespeare goes to some trouble to establish Goneril and Regan as a single evil force: Regan's first words are "I am made of that self mettle as my sister, / And prize me at her worth" (I.i.69−70); the first scene ends with a dialogue in which they agree to act together and which is constructed less as a conversation than as a monologue for two speakers. As the play progresses, they earn the joint title "unnatural hags," but we come to recognize Goneril's superior intelligence and managerial skill and to see that Regan trails behind her, compensating for dullness with exaggerated brutality. By Act V, when their mutual antagonism has become the most virulent in the play, Goneril and Regan are surely no longer a single unit; but in their squabble over Edmund they again seem interchangeable to us (one has to think a moment to remember which sister is murdered and which is the suicide).

A pair of characters who are nearly indistinguishable and also at odds is no more unusual than a pun on *crab* is; consider Tweedledum, Tweedledee, Fafner and Fasolt. My point in bringing up the two equation problems is that they support the assertion that almost any pair of elements one looks at in this play will reveal the essential characteristic of art: like two rhymed words, two verse lines, two metric feet, or two syllables, they will be alike in at least one respect and different in at least one other. That characteristic exercises the mind; when a seemingly infinite number of its manifestations are superimposed on one another as they are in *Lear,* the mind senses that it has reached or perhaps passed the limits of its endurance. Moreover, likeness unifies like elements, isolates them from others, gives them an identity; difference divides. Like "crab" and "crab," Goneril and Regan are a unit and are also detached elements free to relate with or oppose any others. All of which is to say that, as *King Lear* is a giant amplification of the principle of simultaneous likeness and difference, unity and division, its primary quality—the sense it gives both of defined identity and of limitless amorphousness—is only a variation on, and extension of, that principle.

As is always the case with Shakespeare, his techniques in *Lear* are unique only in their degree and density of manifestation. The practice of "rhyming" a pair of sharply contrasted characters by having them share some identifying characteristic is not unusual in literature and is common in Shakespeare; the juggernaut loquacity of Hotspur and Falstaff and Edmund's and Lear's prayers to nature are examples. The names Edmund and Edgar are disquieting variants on the same technique (I doubt that I am alone in the habit for forgetting which name goes with which brother and in feeling foolish even to have approached a confusion between such opposites).[22] In a quite different way, Edgar's disguises make us uneasy about an identity of which we are certain; we are party to the disguises from the beginning, but as they proliferate and Edgar shifts from persona to persona we are simultaneously Edgar's confidants and as disoriented as Gloucester is when he observes (as audiences usually do not) that by IV.vi Edgar has ceased to talk like a Bedlam beggar: "Methinks thy voice is altered, and thou speak'st / In better phrase and matter than thou didst" (7–8).

A similar sense that we lack a hold on categories and that categories lack the power to hold reality results from the unexpectedly literal truth of "Edgar I nothing am" (II.iii.21). Even though Edgar's asides to the audience remind us that this mad beggar is only Edgar in disguise, Poor Tom—perhaps the most thoroughly documented briefly assumed identity in literature—seems more Edgar's fellow character than his persona, and we usually think of him as such (witness the critics who talk about what Poor Tom does or says, but would never speak so of Caius, Cesario, Sir Topas the curate, Friar Lodowick, Old Stanley, or Mr. Premium).

As the identities of the characters in *King Lear* are both firm and perfectly fluid, so are the bases on which we evaluate them. The play asks us to value faithful service, but we are likely to be discomfited when—in IV.v and at his death in IV.vi—the contemptible Oswald turns out to be as selflessly faithful to Goneril as the Fool and Kent are to Lear, and when the peasant who lunges out of the background to act our will by trying to save Gloucester's eyes prefaces his fatal attack on Cornwall by announcing that he has served Cornwall ever since he was a child (III.vii.73).

Values that an audience carries with it everywhere but that are not central to *Lear* are also baffled. Stop for a minute and ask yourself in simple-minded terms whether the battle in Act V is won by the good side or the bad side. This is a battle between the French and the English. The French, whose "secret feet" have been ominously abroad in the land since III.i, lose to our side, the English. This is a battle between the armies of Goneril and Regan, on the one hand, and Lear and Cordelia, on the other; our side loses. The whole problem is further complicated by Albany—of whom it is said that "what most he should dislike seems pleasant to him; / What like, offensive" (IV.ii. 10−11), and who of all the characters in *Lear* is most like its audience, and who wrestles with and mires himself in the muddle of political and moral values (V.i.21−27): Albany simultaneously fights against and on behalf of Lear and Cordelia.

In the first few minutes of *King Lear* a Renaissance audience received signals from which it would have identified the kind of play to follow, predicted its course and the value system it would observe (indeed, Edgar and some critics hope that the play that does follow really is of the kind signaled). First, the audience meets a spiritually brutal old man who jokes boastfully about his past whoring. The Gloucester plot is poised to go the exemplary way of its source, Sidney's *Arcadia* (five hundred pages of lustful strawmen who are crippled by infatuation and brought to grief because they are governed by passion and forget the obligations and aspirations toward which reason beckons them in vain). Any member of a Renaissance audience would have been ready to see Gloucester's subsequent career as a demonstration that "the dark and vicious place" where Gloucester begot his bastard "cost him his eyes," but Shakespeare gave his audience no chance to do so. Our sense of Gloucester's condition changes repeatedly: first we see him as a casually cruel old rake, then in I.ii as a doddering fool, and finally as a pure victim. When Edgar accounts for Gloucester's fate by moralizing the dark and vicious begetting of Edmund, the comment is as insufficient and trivial a summary of what we have seen as it is inappropriate and flat in the dramatic situation in V.iii at the moment Edgar speaks it.

Shakespeare so far expands the range in which the characters and their actions ask to be considered that no system for comprehending them can hold them. But he does not let us altogether abandon any of the frames of reference that the play overlays. In Edgar's desperate efforts to classify and file human experiences, Shakespeare tantalizes us with the comfort to be had from ideologically Procrustean beds to which he refuses to tailor his matter.

The strongest signal Shakespeare gave his audience of coming events and the evaluations appropriate to them is Lear's plan to give up rule and divide his kingdom: this play will be another *Gorboduc*. Lear's action will be the clear cause of clear results in which we will recognize another illustrated exposition of the domino theory of Elizabethan politics. The theory, now best known from Ulysses' lecture on degree (*Troilus and Cressida,* I.iii.125−34), got its most exhaustive theatrical exposition from Thomas Sackville and Thomas Norton, whose urgently homiletic *Gorboduc* appeared almost half a century before Shakespeare wrote *King Lear*.

The undeniable likeness between *Lear* and *Gorboduc*—in both of which the action is precipitated by a legendary English king who divides his kingdom and parcels it out to his children—has been scrupulously demonstrated by Barbara Heliodora Carneiro de Mendonça ("The Influence of *Gorboduc* on *King Lear*," *Shakespeare Survey* 13 [1960]: 41−48); she argues that Shakespeare had *Gorboduc* in mind when he wrote *King Lear*. Whether that is true or not, the beginning of *King Lear* would surely have reminded its audience of the kind of exemplum *Gorboduc* is. An audience's experience of an exemplum is relaxing. Each act of *Gorboduc* begins with a dumb show, an allegorical abstract of the ideas to be embodied in the ensuing action, and closes with a flatfooted and redundant choral interpretation of both the dumb show and the events of the story. The redundancy exists because every action clearly relates to the one frame of philosophical reference it was chosen to serve and because the authors provide characters to moralize the action as it unfolds. All three of the following sample quotations (from vol. 1 of *Drama of the English Renaissance,* ed. Russell A. Fraser and Norman Rabkin [New York, 1976] appear within one short stretch of *Gorboduc:*

> And oft it hath been seen where nature's course
> Hath been perverted in disordered wise,
> When fathers cease to know that they should rule,
> The children cease to know they should obey.
> And often overkindly tenderness
> Is mother of unkindly stubbornness.

> [I.ii. 205−10]

Only I mean to show, by certain rules
Which kind hath graft within the mind of man,
That nature hath her order and her course,
Which being broken, doth corrupt the state
Of minds and things, even in the best of all.

[218—22]

Within one land one single rule is best.
Divided reigns do make divided hearts . . .[23]

[259—60]

For an audience brought up to expect reference to chaos when degree is shaken (conditioned, much as American movie audiences once were to obligatory discussion of universal suffrage whenever any fiction came within hailing distance of political philosophy), Lear's abdication and the partition of his kingdom would have called for commentaries similar to these from *Gorboduc;* but Shakespeare does not provide them—at least he does not provide them in a way calculated to give an audience the comfortable irresponsibility of a secure point of view.

The philosophical platitudes a Renaissance audience learned in school and was ready to apply to *King Lear* are voiced—but only as the maunderings of a superstitious dodderer:

These late eclipses in the sun and moon portend no good to us. Though the wisdom of nature can reason it thus and thus, yet nature finds itself scourged by the sequent effects. Love cools, friendship falls off, brothers divide. In cities, mutinies; in countries, discord; in palaces, treason; and the bond cracked 'twixt son and father. This villain of mine comes under the prediction, there's son against father; the King falls from bias of nature, there's father against child. We have seen the best of our time. Machinations, hollowness, treachery, and all ruinous disorders follow us disquietly to our graves.

[I.ii.101—12]

Here are all the raw materials of the predictable catalogue of predictable aberrations set off by a violation of the natural hierarchy, but an audience in any period is readier to scorn an old wives' tale of astrological influence than it is to scorn the attribution of a similar chain of aberrations to a precipitating human action with which some of the ensuing events are in a demonstrable cause-and-effect relationship. Here Gloucester recognizes and articulates the repeating patterns that we ourselves have observed (Lear and his daughters, Gloucester and his sons; Lear and Kent; Lear and Cordelia, Gloucester and Edgar) and will perceive later (the storm will be to the order of physical nature as Lear was when he disarranged the order of society); but Gloucester's organization of our thoughts disorders them—makes us more, rather than less, uneasy mentally—because the kind of comment we expect to hear and the kind of thinking we ourselves are doing are so distorted by the focus and context Gloucester gives them that they function only as evidence of Gloucester's gullibility. Moreover, even that is not quite straightforward, because Gloucester joins us in recognizing Lear's blindness about Cordelia but is himself blind to Edmund's wickedness and Edgar's virtue. The only mental satisfaction we have in the scene comes from joining the villainous Edmund in the superiority given him by his perspicacity about the mental weakness of his victim—whose fuddled state and patterns of thought are parodies of our own.

An audience's experience with more purely local ideological stances —those evoked in the course of this particular play—is no easier. For example, consider the complexities of thinking about (1) Lear's retinue of knights; (2) Goneril's assessment of it as "riotous," "insolent," and a "disordered rabble" (I.iii. 6, I.iv. 192, 246); and (3) the disguised Kent as one of its members. We know that Kent is noble-spirited; in fact, at the point in *King Lear* when he reappears in disguise to serve where he stands condemned (I.iv. 1−7), Kent is the one major character whom an audience can effortlessly accept as altogether admirable. We also "know" that Lear's hundred knights are unjustly maligned by Goneril; we know so because Goneril is wicked by generic definition, because she admits to Oswald that she seeks to stimulate culpable behavior in Lear's followers (I.iii. 22−25), because the reasons she gives Albany for dismissing the hundred knights have nothing to do with the knights' personal behavior (I.iv. 313−18), and—most importantly—because the one representative knight we meet while Lear is Goneril's guest fully justifies Lear's angry rejoinder to Goneril's accusations: "Detested kite, thou liest. / My train are men of choice and rarest parts" (I.iv. 253−54). The knight is not only notably civil and decorous himself but particularly sensitive to incivility and indecorum in others:

> *Knight.* My lord, I know not what the matter is; but to my judgment
>   your Highness is not entertained with that ceremonious affection as

you were wont. There's a great abatement of kindness appears as well
in the general dependants as in the Duke himself also and your
daughter.

Lear. Ha? Say'st thou so?

Knight. I beseech you pardon me, my lord, if I be mistaken; for my duty
cannot be silent when I think your Highness wronged.

[I.iv.55−63]

The second of the knight's speeches quoted above is, in fact, a
gracious and particularly mannerly restatement of the principle Kent
put forward to justify the honorable insolence for which he was
banished (I.i.145−49, 155−57). Kent himself, however, is—in his
disguise as Lear's recruited retainer, Caius—the only one of Lear's
retinue who displays the wonted behavior Goneril attributed to the
others before Kent joined them. We applaud Kent when he trips
Oswald, but the action we see is an example of just the kind of
bluff, cheerful brutality that one would expect from the entourage
Goneril describes—the entourage we know is otherwise than her
malice would have it be. Later—before Gloucester's house—the admirable, honorable Kent picks a fight with the despicable Oswald.
Oswald speaks politely; Kent responds with a gratuitous lie (he is *not*
of Gloucester's house), and then with clumsy, contrived, and increasingly shrill abuse:

Oswald. Good dawning to thee, friend. Art of this house?

Kent. Ay.

Oswald. Where may we set our horses?

Kent. I' th' mire.

Oswald, Prithee, if thou lov'st me, tell me.

Kent. I love thee not.

Oswald. Why then, I care not for thee.

Kent. If I had thee in Lipsbury Pinfold, I would make thee care for me.

Oswald. Why dost thou use me thus? I know thee not.

Kent. Fellow, I know thee.

Oswald. What dost thou know me for?

Kent. A knave, a rascal, an eater of broken meats; a base, proud,
shallow, beggarly, three-suited, hundred-pound, filthy worsted-
stocking knave; a lily-livered, action-taking, whoreson, glass-
gazing, superserviceable, finical rogue . . .

[II.ii.1−17]

We, of course, know Oswald too: no henchman of Goneril's gets
any sympathy from us. Moments later, moreover, Oswald earns the

contempt that any fictional character evokes from any audience that sees him refuse to "fight like a man." However—and even though Kent later explains why he was then freshly irritated with Oswald (II.iv.26−44)—Oswald's *local* innocence of any crime to justify an attack on him makes our delight in his humiliation less easy to revel in than we would like.

Similarly contradictory responses make it similarly difficult for an audience to maintain its altogether just prejudices during the rest of the scene. We fully accept the justice of Kent's opinions, but what we hear is crude, childish, wilfully perverse insolence to Regan, to Cornwall (who—so far—is guilty only of being Regan's husband and who, like Albany in I.iv, is principally concerned to find out what all the fuss is about), and to the grandly villainous but here unexceptionable Edmund (who speaks only one line in the scene—"How now? What's the matter? Part!" [II.ii.40], and is thereupon grandiloquently challenged by Kent, who shares none of our privileged knowledge of Edmund's villainy—"With you, goodman boy, if you please! Come, I'll flesh ye; come on, young master" [II.ii.41−42]).

The incidental mental discomfort we feel when we see the virtuous Kent in the wrong in minor matters, see the malicious, lying Oswald wronged, and see isolated evidence that could seem to confirm what we took to be—and *still* must take to be—a slander on Lear's hundred knights gets its particular power from the very fact that it *is* incidental. The discomfort I have described disturbs our mental equilibrium but—because it is generated in relation to relatively minor particulars (and as an understandable by-product of the process whereby we become familiar with the purposefully un-Kent-like persona in which Kent disguises himself)—never threatens really to throw our thinking off balance and become a "problem" for interpreters of the play.

As commentators have often observed, perception of moral scale is an essential element in an audience's experience of *King Lear.* The conflict between the most vital responses the play evokes—the conflict between our response to the smug, petty autocrat Lear is in scene i and our responses to him thereafter—has a real but relatively inefficient likeness to the incidental conflicts the play evokes during Kent's first few scenes as Caius the bullyboy. We yearn to see Lear get his comeuppance, but his just deserts are followed by additional

punishments out of all proportion to his crime. We cannot comfortably tell ourselves that "he brought it on himself"—even though he
did. The need to reason the discrepancy between our feelings about
Lear during scene i and those evoked by the subsequent action arises, I
think, only when we look back at the play during a discussion of it.

As we read *King Lear* and as it passes before us in the theatre, the
circumstances of our thinking shift gradually in response to the sequence of events. Lear leaves the stage at line 266 of scene i. When he
reappears at the beginning of scene iv, he is still confidently absolute
("Let me not stay a jot for dinner"), but, though nothing has happened to change Lear's view of his situation, a lot has happened to
change ours: we have heard Cordelia's dire (and generically bolstered)
predictions (I.i.268—75, 280—81); we have heard the wicked sisters
conspire in the last lines of I.i; and scenes ii and iii have focused on
children scheming to undo their parents. By the time we see Lear's
first frustrated confrontation with Oswald, we are ready to see Lear's
situation from Lear's point of view.

The change in our estimate of Lear does not threaten us with
mental crisis and therefore differs greatly from our experiences with
the disguised Kent. Our effortless decision to ally ourselves with Lear
is, however, enhanced by nervous energy generated by incidental and
ultimately weak challenges to our justifiably firm general estimates of
Goneril, Regan, and—especially—Cordelia. Those estimates are jos-
tled by perceptions that could lead to contrary estimates but are
evoked in a moral scale lesser than the one in which we have earlier
assessed the sisters' motives and actions. We are pressed toward, *but
not to,* the point of rethinking and justifying our evaluations.

We are similarly pressed by our experience of the disguised Kent
and by comparably disquieting experiences that arise from the fact
that the wicked Edmund (for whom we felt sympathy in the first
moments of the play during a conversation that ignored his rights and
needs and, in a different dimension, ignored ours as well) takes us
into his confidence and is superficially but intensely attractive when
he does so; and from the fact that the virtuous, philosophical, and
equally confidential Edgar is so often so foolish in his easy, inadequate
moralizing, and from the fact that he so inadequately explains his
tactics in denying his father the comfort of knowing that one of his
sons cares for him. But our best-grounded judgments on Kent, Ed-

mund, and Edgar easily overwhelm the incidental static that complicates our perception of them.

The same is true of the interaction between our first and definitive
moral verdicts on the three sisters and minor irritants to our mental
comfort while we listen to them in scene i. The irritants are too small
to put our judgments of Goneril, Regan, and Cordelia in doubt but
are sufficient to make us peripherally uneasy about our capacity to get
and keep a fixed grip on things.

Consider the incidental awkwardness of listening to the conversation that concludes scene i. Through most of the scene we have been
ready for some summary comment more diagnostically precise than
Kent's hyperbolic "Lear is mad." When the observations we ourselves
have made of "the unruly waywardness that infirm and choleric years
bring with them" (I.i.297−98) are finally given voice, our spokes-
women are the two characters from whom we most wish to be disas-
sociated: Goneril and Regan.

Earlier Cordelia has been our agent in labeling the two fairy-tale
wicked sisters for what they are. Western culture is genetically inca-
pable of producing an audience not conditioned to identify itself with
the youngest of three sisters and to recognize transparent vessels of
wickedness in elder sisters pleasing to their parent. In any case,
Cordelia's first line, an aside, must inevitably fix her in the bosom of
her confidants, the audience: "What shall Cordelia speak? Love, and
be silent" (I.i.62). I am certain that no audience has ever genuinely
changed its mind about Cordelia or felt really tempted to do so. That
would be considerably simpler than what I believe does happen.
When Cordelia's turn comes to bid in Lear's auction, she voices our
contempt for the oily speeches of Goneril and Regan and for the
premises behind the whole charade. We are relieved to hear the
bubbles pricked, but Cordelia's premises do not present a clear antith-
esis to the faults in Lear's. Her ideas are only a variation on Lear's;
she too thinks of affection as a quantitative, portionable medium of
exchange for goods and services (I.i.95−104). Moreover, she sounds
priggish. When she parries Lear's "So young, and so untender? with
"So young, my lord, and true," we share her triumph and her right-
eousness. We exult with her, but we may well be put off by the cold
competence of our Cinderella. We agree with Kent when he says that
she thinks justly and has "most rightly said" (I.i.183), but we are

probably much more comfortable with his passionate speeches on her behalf than we were with her own crisp ones. Cordelia does not *sound* like a victim.[24]

She is silent during Kent's criticisms of Lear; she does not speak again until the suitors are informed of her fall from grace. Shakespeare might then have had her say, *I yet beseech your Majesty that you make known it is no vicious blot, murder or foulness, no unchaste action or dishonored step, that hath deprived me of your grace and favor.* Instead, he laces the speech with gibes at the elder sisters and smug expressions of self-righteousness. Cordelia is justified in all that she says, but not loveable:

> *I yet beseech your Majesty,*
> If for I want that glib and oily art
> To speak and purpose not since what I well intend
> I'll do't before I speak, *that you make known*
> *It is no vicious blot, murder or foulness,*
> *No unchaste action or dishonored step,*
> *That hath deprived me of your grace and favor;*
> But even for want of that for which I am richer—
> A still-soliciting eye, and such a tongue
> That I am glad I have not, though not to have it
> Hath lost me in your liking.
>
> [I.i.223–33; italics mine]

Our discomfort reaches a high point just before Cordelia begins her two-hour absence from the stage. France tells Cordelia to bid her sisters farewell, whereupon Shakespeare gives her two speeches (I.i.268–75, 280–82), that make Lear's peril vivid for us ("The jewels of our father, with washed eyes / Cordelia leaves you") and make Cordelia sound cold, priggish in the extreme, and a bit cheap in the crudeness of her ironies. We find ourselves in perfect agreement with Cordelia's every action and word—and probably also sensible of sharing Regan's irritation when she says, "Prescribe not us our duty" (I.i.276).

As commonly in Shakespeare's plays, the characters in *Lear* apply theatrical metaphors to the events of the fiction in which they are actors in both that word's pertinent senses (see, for example, I.ii.130–31: "and pat he comes, like the catastrophe of the old comedy. My cue is villainous melancholy"; and V.ii.89, Goneril's scornful "An interlude!"). In *King Lear* the metaphors are especially appropriate because the play as play—as an event in the lives of its audience—is analogous to the events it describes. Many commentators have observed that Lear presents the love auction in scene i as a theatrical pageant, a ceremonial enactment of events already concluded: in the first speeches of the play, Gloucester and Kent already know the details of the division, and, when Lear invites Cordelia to speak, he has already assigned all of the kingdom but the opulent third reserved for her. But, like Shakespeare's play, Lear's pageant does not unfold as expected.

Moreover, Shakespeare's audience is like Lear. Even before Shakespeare displays the embryo of a *Gorboduc-Cinderella* hybrid, we have already begun to act like Lear. The first words of the play focus our attention on Albany and Cornwall; as the play progresses, a series of beckoning hints of a coming clash between the two dukes (II.i.10−11, 25−27; III.i.19−29) misleads us down a path to nowhere and does nothing to prepare us for the conflict between the two duchesses.[25] More obviously symptomatic of our Lear-likeness are the character assessments we make during the conversation about Edmund's bastardizing (I.i.7−32). A moment later an audience will instantly assess Lear and join him in evaluating his three children on the basis of a few words; the audience will evaluate the children correctly; Lear will evaluate them incorrectly. The audience will evaluate the father correctly but inadequately. And the audience will be contemptuous of Lear's faith in conclusions reached on such meagre, arbitrarily limited evidence. What we see Lear do during the test is what all audiences do always; what is more, before *this* audience first meets Lear, it has already made character assessments as faulty as Lear's. The division scene echoes the details of the opening conversation in which a casually autocratic parent ("He hath been out nine years, and away he shall again"—I.i.31−32) evaluates his children ("I have a son, sir, by order of law, some year elder than this who yet is no dearer in my account"—18−19). Gloucester's early speeches invite their audience to register him as a brutal oaf (an accurate but insufficient estimate) and Edmund as the humbly patient victim of his father's insensitivity (as erroneous an estimate as Lear's of Goneril and Regan).

Even our evaluations of the play are unfixed. Whenever we find fault with something Shakespeare does in *King Lear,* the alternative turns out to be in some way less acceptable. The plotting of *King Lear* invites adverse criticisms, but what Lear says to Kent on the heath might well be said to anyone who accepts even the more obvious of the invitations:

> Thou'dst shun a bear;
> But if thy flight lay toward the roaring sea,
> Thou'dst meet the bear i' th' mouth.
>
> [III.iv.9—11]

Take, for example, the usually disturbing behavior of Edgar, who seems to be torturing his father by not revealing his identity: when Edgar at last does reveal his identity, the news kills Gloucester instantly. The crowning example, of course, is the end of the play—where we wish events otherwise than they are and where remedy would give more discomfort than the disease.

King Lear turns out to be faithless to the chronicle accounts of Lear, but its perfidy is sudden; the movement of the plot is toward a happy ending. I expect that every audience has felt the impulses that drove Nahum Tate to give *Lear* its promised end and led Samuel Johnson to applaud the deed. But Tate, who called Shakespeare's play "a Heap of Jewels, unstrung, and unpolished," made wholesale changes; after he had strung and polished the treasure he had seized, he had a new heap of jewels altogether. I doubt that many audiences could feel comfortable with a production that made sensible revision of the ending but left the play otherwise as Shakespeare wrote it. Rather than "rise better pleased from the final triumph of persecuted virtue," such an audience would probably value finality above triumph, and echo Kent:

> Vex not his ghost. O, let him pass! He hates him
> That would upon the rack of this tough world
> Stretch him out longer.
>
> [V.iii.314—16]

To allow Lear and Cordelia to retire with victory and felicity would be to allow *more* to occur, would be to allow the range of our consideration and of our standards of evaluation to dilate infinitely. It would be a strong man whose natural ideas of justice and hopes for a happy resolution could outweigh his more basic need—his simple need of an ending—if, instead of Tate, he had seen Shakespeare.

INTERLUDE:
LIKENESSES AND DIFFERENCES
BETWEEN
LOVE'S LABOR'S LOST
AND *KING LEAR*,
COMEDY AND TRAGEDY

The foregoing discussion insists—I think justly—that the manifold inconclusiveness of *King Lear* makes it unique, but I have so far neglected to acknowledge the fact that neither Shakespeare's fascination with indefinition nor the various particular devices by which he exercises and strains his audience's faith in finality are by any means unique to *King Lear*. To take only the largest manifestation of inconclusiveness, consider the precedent of *Love's Labor's Lost:* a comedy of courtship diverted from its course in its final moments, when a messenger interrupts the merriment to report the death of the King of France. My discussion has also ignored the fact that the devices I dwell on are essentially comic.[1] I propose to make up for those omissions now.

Throughout his career, Shakespeare risks the mental well-being of his audiences, exposes his audiences to strenuous demands on their comprehension. Those demands—which range in scale from puns and malapropisms to Shylock and Prospero—are of a kind, a kind by which categories, limits, the very idea of "kind"—in short, the bases of mental well-being—are demonstrated to be arbitrary, artificial, and frail. The categories in which audiences, by virtue of their status *as* audiences, put their greatest faith, and upon which they are necessarily most reliant, are literary ones. Generic signals, a writer's most dependable tools, establish opportune scaffolds on which Shakespeare exercises and investigates the conditioned reflexes by which we take contextual probabilities for certainties. Early in his career, he devoted an entire play, *Love's Labor's Lost,* to exercising those reflexes, frustrating them, and stretching his audience's capacities to survive a series of substantively trivial but nonetheless real exhibitions of the folly of relying on artificial, arbitrary limits.[2]

In *Love's Labor's Lost* the inadequacy of machinery for limiting is basic to the fiction (Navarre's cloistered "little academe" and its rules are breached within moments after they are established) and is persistently demonstrated in the play's language (both in profuse punning and in larger and more disconcerting failures of situational idiom like V.ii.219–20—a sentence that perversely veers from its generically

inevitable conclusion: "Since you are strangers and come here by
chance, / We'll not be nice: take hands—we will not dance"). At the
end of *Love's Labor's Lost,* when two different groups of characters offer
dramatic presentations that do not turn out as their performers expect, Shakespeare explicitly demonstrates, and remarks on, the frailty
of literary genre: he brings his own play to a conclusion extravagantly
foreign to the one toward which he has so predictably progressed, and
he has Berowne—a character *in* the fiction—use a play unfaithful to
its genre as a metaphor for the frustrated action dramatized in *Love's
Labor's Lost,* the "real-life" action in which Berowne is engaged:

> *Berowne.* Our wooing doth not end like an old play;
>   Jack hath not Jill. These ladies' courtesy
>   Might well have made our sport a comedy.
> *King.* Come, sir, it wants a twelvemonth and a day,
>   And then 'twill end.
> *Berowne.*   That's too long for a play.
>
>   [V.ii.864–68]

The same concerns and the same audacity in presenting them recur
in *King Lear.* As it was in *Love's Labor's Lost,* the questionable validity
of promissory sequences of conventional signals is again a topic of the
play. For example, in the second scene of *King Lear* Shakespeare
remarks again, though less directly, on the wonderful, arbitrary neat-
ness of plays. Edmund, having successfully gulled his father, solilo-
quizes on the folly of believing in astrology—the folly of presuming
that certain signs both foretell and determine certain conclusions.
Then, when he is about to shift his focus from his superstitious father
to his brother, Edmund mentions Edgar's name; Edgar enters; and
Edmund smoothly continues his soliloquy with a Pseudolus-like
comment on the fiction-like fitness by which Edgar has arrived on
cue: "and pat he comes, like the catastrophe [i.e., the *conclusion*],[3] of
the old comedy" (I.ii.130). Moreover, although the theatrical analogy is never explicit in scene i, the ceremony of questions, answers,
and predetermined rewards—a pageant staged by Lear with a
playwright's confidence in the sequence of its events—is openly play-
like and becomes ironically so when Cordelia refuses to speak in
response to her cue.[4]

    As I suggested earlier, the fabric of *Love's Labor's Lost* is, like the
fabric of *King Lear,* permeated with demonstrations of indefiniteness.

The largest fact of the work—its failure to reach its generically ap-
pointed end—is manifested in its smallest elements. For instance, the
very sentence that diverts the play from proceeding to its generically
signaled end both echoes the form it imposes on the whole (Marcade
never gets to finish the sentence) and, in the Princess's here-justified
confidence in contextual probabilities, demonstrates exactly the
semiotic phenomenon that causes us to be surprised when, unlike
Marcade's sentence, *Love's Labor's Lost* turns out not to intend the
conclusion it signals:

> *Enter a Messenger, Monsieur Marcade.*
> *Marcade.* God save you, madam.
> *Princess.* Welcome, Marcade;
>   But that thou interrupt'st our merriment.
> *Marcade.* I am sorry, madam, for the news I bring
>   Is heavy in my tongue. The king your father—
> *Princess.* Dead, for my life!
> *Marcade.* Even so, My tale is told.
>
> [V.ii.705—11]

In supporting the proposition that uneasiness about endings presents itself in every aspect of *Love's Labor's Lost,* I will, as I did when I
discussed the manifold indefinition in *King Lear,* again insist on the
likeness of—and the relationship among—indefinitenesses manifested in such things as failure to conclude, failure to reach an
expected kind of conclusion, failure of characters to abide by the
common-law rules for their generic types, and awkward interaction
between set speeches or stock verbal formulas and situations that do
not fit them. Here, then, is a representative fraction of the evidence
in *Love's Labor's Lost* of Shakespeare's concern about definition in all
its aspects.

To start with a merely theatrical example, consider the fact that
Love's Labor's Lost is unique among Shakespeare's plays in never once
providing a graceful exit from the stage for any of its characters (for
extreme instances, look at Jaquenetta's exits). For a distantly related
example of the play's general insistence upon straining and questioning the easy (but rigid and therefore brittle) limitations upon which
dramatic performances rely, consider the simultaneously reasonable
and variously unreasonable emendations Moth makes in his carefully

rehearsed set speech when the ladies whose eyes his speech praises turn
their backs on him:

> *Enter Blackamoors with music;* [*Moth,*] *the Boy, with a speech, and the rest*
> *of the Lords disguised.*
> *Moth.* All hail, the richest beauties on the earth!
> *Boyet.* Beauties no richer than rich taffeta.
> *Moth.* A holy parcel of the fairest dames,
>   *The Ladies turn their backs to him.*
>   That ever turned their—backs—to mortal views!
> *Berowne.* 'Their eyes,' villain, 'their eyes.'
> *Moth.* That ever turned their eyes to mortal views!
>   Out—
> *Boyet.* True. 'Out' indeed.
> *Moth.* Out of your favors, heavenly spirits, vouchsafe
>   Not to behold—
> *Berowne.* 'Once to behold,' rogue.
>
> [V.ii.158—68]

Armado's objection to casting Moth as Hercules—whom one ordinarily thinks of as an adult—and Holofernes's sensible but mechanical
solution to the problem (V.i.116—23) present a related example of
casual examination into our reliance on frail, arbitrary, convenient,
altogether insubstantial limits.

  For an example in another dimension entirely, consider the conclusions Costard presses on other speakers' sentences. He fills them out
with tags that follow locally irrelevant signals of phrasing and entirely
ignore the purposes toward which the speaker's logic is moving:

> *King.* Peace!
> *Costard.* Be to me and every man that dares not fight.
> *King.* No words!
> *Costard.* Of other men's secrets, I beseech you.
>
> [I.i.220—23]

Jaquenetta's "witty" responses to Armado (I.ii. 130—34: "With that
face?"; "So I heard you say"; "Fair weather after you!") are chosen
with similar and similarly improbable arbitrariness; her snappy replies—apparently traditional among peasant sophisticates—respond
to her ambition to sound sharp and superior rather than to the particulars of the context in which she speaks them.

The longest sustained and most various attack on an audience's assumptions about limits is in the planning and performance of the pageant of the Nine Worthies. When *Love's Labor's Lost* was new, its audience might have been incidentally and casually puzzled by Shakespeare's and/or Holofernes's choice in specifying *the* Nine Worthies. Shakespeare's plays so dominate the formal and informal education of English speakers that we usually have our first knowledge of any Shakespearean topic or device from Shakespeare. For instance, our norms for the stories of Richard III and Octavius Caesar are Shakespeare's versions. So, too, we must work hard not to take traditional vices and disguised pastoral heroines as variants on Iago and Rosalind. As it is ordinarily a surprise to modern students to hear that in all tellings before Shakespeare's the story of Lear had a fairy-tale happy ending, so we are likely to know of the Nine Worthies only from Shakespeare, to take the six specified in *Love's Labor's Lost* as traditional, and to forget the harmless pedantry by which scholarly footnotes tell us that *Love's Labor's Lost* is the only place where Pompey and Hercules make the list. Audiences familiar with the "Worthy" tradition may well have been slightly uncomfortable with the list Holofernes gives—not, I think, uncomfortable at deviation from a loose tradition that always included some "either/or" selections, but uncomfortable about bothering to note the oddity of a list presented by so purely ridiculous a character as Holofernes—uncomfortable about catching themselves behaving just like the pointlessly punctilious Holofernes himself.[5]

Speculation on that peculiarly convoluted thought process is warranted because the pageant of the Worthies invokes similar problems for the characters in *Love's Labor's Lost* and is likely to evoke similar problems for audiences whether they know about the Worthies or not. All the problems are problems of identity and definition.

Just before the pageant begins, the King and Berowne stop to do tapsters' reckonings on the cast list Armado has presented to them:

> *King.* Here is like to be a good presence of Worthies. He presents
> Hector of Troy; the swain, Pompey the Great; the parish curate,
> Alexander; Armado's page, Hercules; the pedant, Judas Maccabaeus:
> And if these four Worthies in their first show thrive,
> These four will change habits and present the other five.

Berowne. There is five in the first show.

King. You are deceived, 'tis not so.

Berowne. The pendant, the braggart, the hedge-priest, the fool, and the
  boy—
  Abate throw at novum, and the whole world again
  Cannot pick out five such, take each one in his vein.

                                                [V.ii.530—41]

From the beginning, *Love's Labor's Lost* has taken time to dwell
gratuitously upon numbers—particularly three and four. A kind of
uncertainty about numbers is built into the play's structure. The
various confusions about the cast list of the pageant is like a confusion
common among students in classroom discussions and among knowl-
edgeable playgoers I overhear responding to their companions' re-
quests to know "which one's this?" before performances of *Love's
Labor's Lost* at summer Shakespeare festivals. They regularly refer to
the *three* young men who have vowed to study and the *three* young
women they woo. Such errors are, of course, inconsequential, but the
play invites them. The number of years that the four men swear to
study is three, and we see only three swearers (the King acts as master
of ceremonies). In fact, both of the two groups of four are always
groups of one and three, in which the one distinguished from his or
her companions varies as the principle of distinction varies: in terms
of rank, the two groups are the King and his three companions, the
Princess and hers; however, Berowne and Rosaline are more spirited,
wittier, and less ready to cooperate than their cohorts, and the play
often asks us to see the two groups as Berowne and the other three and
Rosaline and the other three.

A different sort of numerical dubiety comes into play in I.ii, when
Moth proposes to understand "to study three years with the duke" as
to study the words *three* and *years*:

Armado. I have promised to study three years with the duke.

Moth. You may do it in an hour, sir.

Armado. Impossible.

Moth. How many is one thrice told?

Armado. I am ill at reckoning; it fitteth the spirit of a tapster.

Moth. You are a gentleman and a gamester, sir.

Armado. I confess both. They are both the varnish of a complete man.

Man. Then, I am sure you know how much the gross sum of deuce-ace
  amounts to.

Armado. It doth amount to one more than two.

Moth. Which the base vulgar do call three.

Armado. True.

Moth. Why, sir, is this such a piece of study? Now here is three studied ere ye'll thrice wink; and how easy is it to put 'years' to the word 'three,' and study three years in two words . . .

[34—52]

Intervening between Armado's statement of his problem and Moth's depreciative solution to it is a passage of incidental posturing by Armado and mockery by Moth (a passage—by the way—that rings casual changes on three and one). During that passage we are invited to laugh not only at Armado's ridiculous affectation but also at the ridiculousness of his choice of matters to be affected about; we scorn Armado for pretending—and bothering to pretend—general class-based superiority to arithmetic: to know and use the multiplication tables is not therefore to resemble a publican figuring up a bill. On the other hand, the King and Berowne seem momentarily foolish when, in Holofernes's own punctilious way, they count the actors who will present Worthies.

The blurred distinction between Holofernes—a burlesque caricature—and the "gentles"—with whom we feel human kinship even though we laugh at their follies as self-cloistered scholars, glib equivocators, and copybook courtly lovers— is one of many by which comfortable dramatic categories are strained. For example, Shakespeare persistently insists on likenesses between Costard and Berowne. Moreover, the play's own kind is several times jarred and momentarily cracked when conversation wanders from light comedy and stumbles upon humanly probable facts and events that the play's genre promises to keep out. One such remarkable detour occurs when the ladies fall unexpectedly into idle chat about the death of Katharine's sister (V.ii. 13 — 15) and is immediately succeeded by another when, having first slid back into elegant banter, Katharine and Rosaline become uncomfortably vigorous and nasty in what the Princess insists is only "a set of wit well played" (V.ii. 15 — 46).

Aside from the great disjunction brought about by Marcade's report of the French King's death, the preeminent example of the play's failure to abide by generic limits is Holofernes's sudden insistence upon his right to be considered as a human being rather than a stick figure. Boyet and the four young men have cooperated heartily in frustrating the Worthies—mocking the pageant and the performers. Holofernes, the governing spirit of the show, gets the harshest treatment and, when the gentlefolk have at last exhausted the punning potential of the name "Judas," Holofernes speaks one of the most moving lines in Shakespeare—a line that remains disturbing even when dutiful actors and directors try to make it sound foolish. Instead of shuffling meekly off like the curate before him, Holofernes says: "This is not generous, not gentle, not humble" (V.ii.621). In an audience's terms, the line registers the fact that the open and openly cruel mockery has broken through the limits that come with the well-born characters' identities as gracious and noble. And the line also explodes the comfortable, literarily common convention by which audiences are used to assuming that clowns and dolts are mere figures of fun and therefore exempt from the sympathy we extend to other fictional characters.

As a focal point for illustrating the degree to which the idea of "the end" pervades *Love's Labor's Lost,* nothing in the play beats the music-hall/burlesque-show routine that erupts when Costard hurts his shin and he, Moth, and Armado discuss the injury. I want to examine the passage closely, not for its own sake but to suggest the degree to which the idea of *the end* possessed Shakespeare's imagination as he wrote the play.

The shin passage (III.i.63 – 123) begins with a joke about the two ends of a human body (*costard* means "apple," but was a slang term for "head"—compare the modern "to be out of one's gourd"): "Here's a costard broken in a shin." From there the conversation follows randomly intersecting phonetic or semantic routes to confusions among the words *enigma, l'envoy* (in Armado's "Some enigma, some riddle. Come thy l'envoy"), *enema, salve, salvo* (a volley of firearms, metaphorically pertinent to an enema), and *salvé* (a salutation on meeting).[6] With typically studied inefficiency, Armado attempts to do what he says a "l'envoy" does: he tries to make his meaning plain (clear); however, he refuses to speak plainly (simply), and therefore runs afoul of Moth's ingenuity (and, in passing, accidentally recurs to Costard's request that his wound be treated only with a plantain leaf—"a plain plantain"):

> *Moth.*   Is not l'envoy a salve?
> *Armado.* No, page; it is an epilogue, or discourse to make plain
>   Some obscure precedence that hath tofore been sain.

I will example it:
> The fox, the ape, and the humble-bee
> Were still at odds, being but three.

There's the moral. Now the l'envoy.

Moth. I will add the l'envoy. Say the moral again.

Armado. The fox, the ape, and the humble-bee
> Were still at odds, being but three.

Moth.   Until the goose came out of door,
> And stayed the odds by adding four.

[73–84]

From there the conversation zig-zags wantonly on—on (1) to demonstrate indefiniteness of effect in literary conclusions ("Now will I begin your moral, and do you follow with my l'envoy . . ." —85–90); (2) to play, as Ellis explains (pp. 57–59), on the coincidence between *-oy,* which is the end of the word "l'envoy"—and *oie,* which is the French word for goose ("A good l'envoy, ending in the goose"—91)[7]—and (since *l'envoy* is not only a French word for postscript but a variant form of the French word for blindworm) to play simultaneously on the fact that, as Ellis says, "should an *envoy,* or slowworm, fall in the way of a goose, it would surely end in the goose" (p. 54); and (3) to luxuriate in the general colloquial potential of the word *goose*: Costard reaches out to allude to the proverbial expression "to sell someone a goose for a bargain" (meaning "to make a fool of him") and to activate bawdy overtones *goose* had by virtue of being a common cant term for whore and—in "Winchester goose"—venereal disease:

The boy hath sold him a bargain, a goose—that's flat.
Sir, your pennyworth is good, an your goose be fat.
To sell a bargain well is as cunning as fast and loose.
Let me see—a fat l'envoy—ay, that's a fat goose.

[93–96]

Now that the tangentially directed banter has gone on for thirty frantic, aimless lines, Armado calls a halt and makes overt acknowledgment of the conversation's *Love's Labor's Lost*-like failure to arrive at a rationally predictable conclusion:

Armado. Come hither, come hither. How did this argument begin?

Moth. By saying that a costard was broken in a shin.
> Then called you for the l'envoy.

> *Costard.* True, and I for a plantain; thus came your argument in;
>   Then the boy's fat l'envoy, the goose that you bought;
>   And he ended the market.
> *Armado.* But tell me, how was there a costard broken in a shin?
>
>   [97 – 104]

Moth and Costard respond; and the topic skitters away again. Armado tries once more to speak to the purpose ("We will talk no more of this matter"), but—after Armado introduces a new topic and a new word, *enfranchise,* to play with—Costard suddenly jumps his hearers back to *l'envoy* and *goose:*

> *Armado.* Sirrah Costard, I will enfranchise thee.
> *Costard.* O, marry me to one Frances! I smell some
>   l'envoy, some goose, in this.
>
>   [112 – 14][8]

Once Armado does get his meaning across, Costard offers one last synonym for *enfranchise* and thus manages one last detour into the verbal-scatological superlogic that has replaced ordinary substantive logic in the conversation:

> *Armado.* By my sweet soul, I mean setting thee at liberty, enfreedom-
>   ing thy person. Thou wert immured, restrained, captivated, bound.
> *Costard.* True, true, and now you will be my purgation and let me
>   loose.
>
>   [115 – 19]

When the characters' lust for punning on *l'envoy* finally subsides, Shakespeare's—the play's—does not; Armado returns to his original purpose: his end in arranging this interview in the first place was to send Costard to Jaquenetta with a letter—to make Costard his envoy.

Before I leave the conversation about Costard's shin, I want to talk generally about the word *goose,* the word Costard and Shakespeare are at such pains to introduce as a synonym for *l'envoy.* Both in the shin passage and throughout the play, the operation of the word *goose* is complex and problematic. The activities of *goose* in *Love's Labor's Lost* are improbably trivial matters for critical concern—especially in context of a highly serious discussion of tragedy. However, since it can materially illustrate my account of Shakespeare's flirtation with indefinition, and since it relates variously to his general concern with ends in *Love's Labor's Lost,* I think that pausing to examine the interactions of various connotations of *goose* will be neither so frivolous nor so digressive as it might seem to be.

For one thing, a pun is the commonest and smallest practical manifestation of the fragility of definitions. Since a word *is* a definer—exists to fix quasi-physical limits to an idea—the experience of perceiving a pun is a real, though admittedly petty, experience of collapsing limits. The wordplay on *goose,* however, cannot exactly be called punning but something similar, more nebulous, and more disquieting to its listeners' equilibrium than the clean, sudden collision of senses and contexts that constitutes a pun.

Geese figure in *Love's Labor's Lost* at two other points—one earlier than the shin passage, one later. The first is in scene i—in another passage emblematic of Shakespeare's preoccupation with conclusions, their arbitrariness, and the frailty of the assumption that *an* organizing principle (in this case, the topic under discussion) will remain exclusive. That passage—a companion piece to the one about the fox, the ape, and the humble bee—is also one in which the conclusion of a quatrain is achieved when geese make a fortuitous entrance. Berowne's three friends comment on the elegant logic chopping by which he has protested the oath on which their little academe is founded:

> *King.* How well he's read to reason against reading!
> *Dumaine.* Proceeded well, to stop all good proceeding!
> *Longaville.* He weeds the corn, and still lets grow the weeding.
> *Berowne.* The spring is near, when green geese are a-breeding.
> *Dumaine.* How follows that?
> *Berowne.*   Fit in his place and time.
> *Dumaine.* In reason nothing.
> *Berowne.*   Something then in rime.
>   [I.i.94–99]

What little semantic pertinence Berowne's geese have to the argument goes to call his three friends fools—geese. But these are *green*geese: *greengoose* was a stock slang term for "whore,"[9] and these greengeese are "breeding." Berowne's substantively impertinent conclusion thus has a feel of sexual double entendre. The reference to greengeese sounds witty, but its wit—like the pertinence of Berowne's line to its context—is merely formal. It *sounds* like an apt, clever, probably stinging allusion and therefore makes real, but substantively unfounded, claim to a special pertinence that offsets its ostentatious *im*pertinence. But—since reference to whores here is, as far as I can see, as entirely unrelated to the situation as reference to barnyard fowl is—the apparently pregnant reference to greengeese presumably goes, and always went, past each particular informed auditor as a joke that he is too slow-witted to fathom. The jokelike non-joke in "greengeese" thus complements and mirrors the physics whereby the whole line formally concludes a quatrain to which it is substantively irrelevant—just as the arbitrarily concluded quatrain is a model of the ultimate shape of *Love's Labor's Lost* at large.[10]

The third and last of the goose references in *Love's Labor's Lost* occurs during the eavesdropping scene; Berowne comments on the sonnet Longaville has written to Maria ("Thou being a goddess, I forswore not thee"): "This is the liver-vein, which makes flesh a deity, / A green goose a goddess" (IV.ii.69–70).[11] Since a green-goose is a young one, a gosling, its use in contrast to a goddess is usually and properly explained as a metaphor for "a gawky young girl," one lately pubescent and troubled with the green-sickness. Here, however, *greengoose* describes an unworthy object of a lover's adoration; a gawky teenager would be unworthy as unattractive; a whore would be unworthy as morally and probably physically un-wholesome. My object here is not to argue for or against either gloss or even to insist that both pertain. I mean only to suggest that the term has a special imprecision—fails, for all its metaphoric spe-cificity, to define its object.

In the lines from which the present wild-goose chase began, Costard's playful cadenza on "fat goose" is plainly obscene—but it is also obscure. The frequency of *goose* in whorish contexts might alone be sufficient to generate the obscenity, but just what that obscenity is is not clear. The context—and this is the principal point toward which this whole excursion has aimed—suggests some reference to buttocks; in equating "a fat envoy" with "a fat goose," Costard pre-sents both terms as if they were synonyms for "a fat arse."[12]

The reason I have gone to such lengths to establish *goose* as a buttock-related word is that references to buttocks (and to excrement) function largely in the play's alliteration-like concern with the topic of ends—terminal points, limits, goals (targets, marks, butts), pur-poses, results, conclusions, and death. The foolish, quarrelsome geese that so persistently furnish conclusions when matters are left at odds in *Love's Labor's Lost* are thus parties to a thought pattern that includes "thou hast it ad dunghill, at the fingers' ends, as they say" (V.i.69), and "the posteriors of this day, which the rude multitude call the afternoon" (V.i.79–80), and "it will please his Grace . . . sometime to lean upon my poor shoulder, and with his royal finger thus dally with my excrement, with my mustachio—but, sweet heart, let that pass" (V.i.91–94).

The culminating example of interaction between a synonym for fool ("ass" being an alternative epithet to "goose"), and a synonym for "buttocks" occurs during Holofernes's appearance as Judas Maccabaeus in his pageant of the Nine Worthies—the cruel "ass"/"arse" joke about the final syllable of "Judas" (a joke that follows and anatomically complements a series of jokes about Holofernes's face and head):

> *Boyet.* Therefore as he is (an ass), let him go.
>   And so adieu, sweet Jude. Nay, why dost thou stay?
> *Dumaine.* For the latter end of his name.
> *Berowne.* For the ass to the Jude? Give it him. Jud-as, away!
>   [V.ii.617–20]

So, to sum up, *Love's Labor's Lost* is so *Lear*-like in its variations on the theme of conclusion that it could—with almost as much justice as ingenuity—be described as a sustained two-hour pun on the word *end*.

Although I believe the likenesses between *Love's Labor's Lost* and *King Lear* are more than superficial, they are obviously trivial compared to differences so obvious and so urgent that a serious comparison of the two plays seems wantonly and perversely nearsighted, an academic parlor trick. There is probably nothing in literature that feels so hugely "consequential" (*consequential* in its popular metaphoric sense) as *King Lear* does. On the other hand, poor little *Love's Labor's Lost* is so *in*consequential that, despite the literal inconsequence of its anticlimactic final solemnity to the generic premises invaded by Marcade, the play still strikes audiences as fluff. The chief difference between *King Lear* and *Love's Labor's Lost* derives from the difference between the physical facts of the stories they dramatize.

That is as true as it is obvious. When I come to discuss *Macbeth,* I will have a lot to say about the relation of events we call tragic and plays we call tragic. I will then suggest a common denominator between the two, a common denominator less obvious and more essential than the one superficially inherent in the fact that the sort of event we call tragic when we read about it in the newspapers, hear about it from the neighbors, or experience it for ourselves is likely to be of the same general sort that is central to the story of a dramatic tragedy. Although everyone who has ever read a plot summary of *King Lear* (or *Macbeth* or *Othello* or *Oedipus Rex*) is aware that—as soap operas, disaster movies, and narrative accounts of terrible events demonstrate—the physical facts of the plot of *King Lear* are not, of themselves, the determining elements that evoke the response we comment on when we say "tragic," I will suggest that our responses to tragic events in real life are evoked by factors in our perceptions of them that also occur in our artist-managed perceptions of the literary works that we label tragedies. If there were call to do so, I would argue the similar but self-evident case for our responses to funny events (e.g., puns or men slipping on banana peels) and the response that causes us to label a particular literary work "comic."

For the moment, however, I am concerned, first, to make it clear that, in undertaking a task as apparently necessary as a demonstration that Arabia is not a lake, I am fully aware of the obvious: it matters a lot that none of the characters we meet in *Love's Labor's Lost* suffers seriously and that, aside from peripheral, forgettable figures like Burgundy, France, and Curan, only three of the characters in *King Lear* survive it. Second, having granted that what happens in their stories precludes a tragic response to *Love's Labor's Lost* and a comic response to *King Lear,* I want to explain why I introduce *Love's Labor's Lost* into a discussion of tragedy: I hope that examination of the differences between the very different effects *King Lear* and *Love's Labor's Lost* evoke by similar means may help toward disposing of a paradox that has troubled me and, if there is any validity to my line of thought, may have troubled other people: the more I thought about the nature of tragedy and the closer I felt myself coming to a definition of tragedy, the closer my generalizations came to defining comedy.

I will now resume discussion of *Love's Labor's Lost* in order to develop a less-than-obvious reason why it is not—as, for other and evident reasons, it could not be—a tragedy.

Love's Labor's Lost seems not only inconsequential but doggedly determined to maintain its inconsequence in the face of its own repeated threats to its audience's generically maintained isolation from the necessity to see—and from opportunities to see—characters and events in the full human perspective in which we ordinarily see and evaluate human events and human behavior. *Love's Labor's Lost* is comparable to a Punch and Judy show—but one that both evokes and dutifully suppresses an audience's altogether inappropriate dismay at onstage infanticide and/or sympathy with a murderer whose pathological violence may be supposed an indirect psychological result of his pathetically hideous physical deformity. By including such things as the ladies' playful chat about the death of the sister of one of them and as Holofernes's just and dignified moral outrage, *Love's Labor's Lost* persistently beckons its audience up dark mental alleys ordinarily hidden from audiences moving, carefree, along the gracefully cut paths of situation comedy. But the play parades confidently along as though oblivious to the fact that its audience's faith in the generic isolation of characters, actions, and situations from consideration in ordinary human terms has faltered—faltered but not fallen. In context of a discussion of *King Lear,* the key fact about *Love's Labor's Lost* is that—when it causes us incidental mental discomfort in passage and when it entirely surprises us at the end—its behavior seems *deviant*.

Although *Love's Labor's Lost* may strike us as truer to artistically unmediated experience than fictions (particularly ostentatiously artificial, painfully wrought fictions) usually are, and truer to life than most of its form-drunken characters expect life to be, the play feels untrue to an unchallenged nature larger than itself—the nature of plays of the kind it tells us it is and promises to persist in being. *Love's Labor's Lost* is a strange play—merely strange. It is, I think, no accident that *funny* has become a working synonym for *strange:* both words register a response rooted in confidence about the unquestionable natural rightness of whatever customary pattern it is that the remarkable isolated instance has violated.

Love's Labor's Lost does not threaten its audience's assumptions about the nature of things—the nature of human experience or the nature of plays. At the end of the play, when Marcade and news of the French king's death intrude upon—and break the boundaries of—elegant comedy and its potential, an audience's sense of the event is, I think, like Berowne's: a sense that the "wooing doth not end like an old play"—that this play has not come out right—that, however solemn his materials, Shakespeare has played a practical joke on us.

Our sense of that ultimate violation of norms in *Love's Labor's Lost* is thus like our sense of the lesser ones that precede it. Like our previous responses, the big last one strengthens our sense of the validity of the violated norm. That is to say that the sudden pall Marcade throws upon both the dramatized situation and the dramatization operates in a way similar to the way jokes work. I do not mean to suggest that there is anything laughable about the eruption of inconvenient possibility that untracks the roller-coaster certainty of the play's progress toward a matrimonial close. I mean only to suggest that our uncomplicated feeling that *Love's Labor's Lost* has not come out right[13] reinforces our confidence that there is a right way to follow, that the play has perversely strayed from a path that is real.

All comedy always and necessarily depends on certainty of what is right and therefore presumes and reinforces our faith in the existence of an evident right way—a right way readily distinguishable from alternative candidates. When we laugh at a deviation from a system we have assumed to be exclusive, we laugh to discover that the system is not exclusive, but we do not doubt that it naturally *should* be so. When a man slips on a banana peel, our faith in a natural order in which setting out to walk from point A to point B delivers the walker smoothly at point B is not shaken but reinforced. Our response is not to heightened consciousness of the flimsiness of the patterns and symptoms on which we rely. We see the banana peel as accidental to the undoubted essence of walkways and the man's sudden collapse as a mere aberration. Anything we laugh at can be similarly analyzed; a pun, for instance, confirms the quasi-physical objective identity of the context it invades; so does a malapropism; and "Because they are not eight" confirms the generically defined conventional limits on the kind of answer that a question like "What is the reason why the seven stars are no more than seven?" can admit. The assumptions by which the word *aberration* has meaning are always confirmed by any event to which we apply it—or apply comfortable, kindred words like *error, perverse, deviate,* and *funny.*

Comedy has traditionally seemed contemptible—at least relatively so as compared with other modes. That that statement is true is vouched for by the fact that, although we may not accept the premises of phrases like "just a comedy," we are not surprised to hear them. The near universality of casual, popular contempt for comedy is also witnessed by the sturdy efforts of generations of Horation literary theorists to end the tradition by persuasive and/or pious arguments for comedy's therapeutic effects. The theorists themselves always sound to me very much as nutritionists sound when they voice their inexhaustible surprise that bananas—which are soft, sweet, and pleasing to children—are actually good for children. Moreover, there is a suspicious shrillness about sanctimoniously reiterated endorsements of a sense of humor as a human virtue—endorsements issued dogmatically by just the kinds of parlor philosophers whose other pronouncements we shrug off as shallow and convenient.

I suggest that the *fact* of anticomic prejudice—a prejudice one can hear in the rhetorical stances even of comedy's most determined champions—is more informative about comedy than efforts to counteract that prejudice have been. However thoughtless the casually bigoted multitude may be in considering comedy trivial, there is a fact behind the prejudice—even if the prejudiced have never consciously perceived it. Comedy, for all its gestures of fearlessness, is not ruthless in admitting truth; it must always rest upon some unexamined assumption. It therefore holds its audience back from the need to recognize the infinity of possibility and the insufficiency of human mental resources to manage unstoppable improbabilities. Mark Twain said that man is the only animal that blushes—or needs to. The same can be said about laughing. Comedy, by its very physics, bullies us into actively exercising a faith in limits. When we laugh, we do not so much exercise mental flexibility as retreat to a bastion at a comfortable distance from the particular point where some particular rigidity has proved brittle. I have always wondered at the good humor of audiences leaving theatres after tragedies and at the curious sullenness I have seen in departing audiences after comedies at which their laughter has been audible in the street outside the theatre. It may be that, whatever we may consciously believe, we feel cheated by comedies and grateful to tragedies.

Since both tragedy and comedy derive from violations of our expectation, the perceptual particulars of the experiences we call tragic turn out to be disconcertingly similar to their counterparts in experiences we call comic. That real but superficial likeness is demonstrated in the following pair of superficially similar propositions and corollaries about "the nature of things" and human folly. The pair also demonstrates the difference I have focused on in contrasting *Love's Labor's Lost* and *King Lear*.

Comedy operates from—and demonstrates—the proposition that there is a way things are and fools forget what it is. Regrettably, however, no one is always or altogether immune from occasional fits of foolish forgetfulness.

Tragedy operates from—and demonstrates—the proposition that there is a way things are and that fools assume it is knowable and known. Regrettably, however, no one is or can be exempt from the moment-to-moment, day-by-day necessity of assuming that the ways of things are as previous experience leads us to expect them to be.

PART II
MACBETH, ARISTOTLE,
DEFINITION, AND TRAGEDY

1. Hold Enough

This essay arises from the following sequence of bland and standard observations made while I was reading criticisms of *Macbeth*. (1) With the possible exception of *King Lear, Macbeth* is more often discussed *as* tragedy than the other tragedies of Shakespeare are. (2) Even though there has been a good deal of attention to defining the distinguishable literary types other than tragedy, one is more likely to see a critic of a particular dramatic tragedy measure it against the demands of a definition of tragedy than one is to see a critic discuss a particular dramatic comedy, or epic, or novel as successful or unsuccessful in meeting a standard of its genre. (3) The search for a definition of tragedy has been the most persistent and widespread of all nonreligious quests for definition. I am drawn toward testing the hypothesis that the urge to define tragedy and the urge to define—that is, the urge to have limits—may be more than obviously related and toward speculating on the significance of the regular concern for various kinds of definitions and limits that is felt by the characters, critics, and, perhaps, audiences of *Macbeth*.

Before succumbing to the draw of those projects, it will be wise to consider the possibility that my three observations are inconsequential and related to one another chiefly as they bear witness to the strength of critical habit and to the power of the precedent of Aristotle's *Poetics*. Particular attention to *Macbeth* as tragedy might be accounted for as a subhabit, engendered by curricular requirements (for the introduction of students to the *Poetics*, to Greek tragedy, and to Shakespeare in a sample convenient to the first two) and nursed by the example of such exercises as R. G. Moulton's abstract of *Macbeth* arranged as a Greek tragedy (*The Ancient Classical Drama*, 1890). The argument for dismissing my three phenomena could be greatly enlarged along these general lines, but my suspicion persists that there is something to be learned from the conjunction of the three.

Tradition will not satisfactorily explain them away. The habit of following Aristotle's lead was, after all, insufficient to maintain him as an oracle on other matters. During the Middle Ages and most of the Renaissance, Aristotle's theories and the "Aristotelian" theories accreted to them had been treated rather like revealed truth. But, after a slow start in the late sixteenth century, Aristotle's unnatural natural science was gradually superseded, first by other theories and then, increasingly, by conclusions inductively derived from observations. There was, of course, no sharp, sudden change in the way people thought, but they became less inclined to take revelations about the things of this world in the same terms that they took divine revelation. Aristotle was not, and is not likely to be, discredited as a thinker; but Aristotle, the source of semidivine revelation about what does not have to be divinely revealed, has lost his place as the fourth member of the Trinity. He lost it in all but one field: we still use Aristotle's dicta on tragedy *in the way* we use a source for truth that, like the revealed truth of the Bible, is not available to human beings at first hand.

That we do so is all the more surprising because the *Poetics* were for all practical purposes unknown during the ascendancy of Aristotle's other work. It was not translated until 1498, and was in no way influential before the middle of the sixteenth century. Even then, the admirers of Aristotle were only lip-servants of their master; the pseudo-Aristotelian tradition—running from Francesco Robortello's commentaries in 1548, through Lodovico Castelvetro's derivation of the infamous unities in 1570, to Boileau in 1674—is a tradition really not even pseudo-Aristotelian but anti-Aristotelian, a tradition of debasement—phrased in Aristotelian echoes—not of Aristotle but of the Horation doctrine of sweetened instruction.

I do not, therefore, think that the live roots of our habit of taking occasional nearly religious recourse to the authority of Aristotle are to be found in the Aristotelianism that led up to and down from Boileau.

Before I go further, I should point out that, as I exclude the French neoclassic pseudo-Aristotelians, their predecessors and their disciples as irrelevant to what I say about our need for a definition of tragedy and our reliance on Aristotle in particular. I also exclude the current school of American (or "Chicago") Aristotelians and, for that matter, all other responsible, sophisticated commentary on the *Poetics* or derived from it. Please understand that I am concerned here neither with seriously Aristotelian criticism nor with the theoreticians who have fleshed out the perceptions recorded in the *Poetics.* I talk about the *Poetics* raw. I do so because most students and critics meet it raw and have ad hoc recourse to *it* and not to the purposeful, systematic Aristotelianism that grew from it. The users of Aristotle I refer to here are wantonly casual and much, much more common among us than real Aristotelian critics are. The users of Aristotle that concern me here are the thousands of fair-weather Aristotelians. They—we —use the *Poetics* as an intellectual life preserver.

The habit of using the *Poetics* to keep one's arguments afloat dates, I think, from the Victorian and Edwardian critics who were not intellectually comfortable about accounting for the greatness of great literature by reducing it to the status of moral demonstration. People like Newman, Quiller-Couch, and Bradley, whose gentleman's education included Greek and reverence for Greek culture, were, I think, sure of the value of literature and sure of the superior value of tragedy to other kinds of literature, but were, like most critics at most times, unsure about the source of that value. Since their time we have never fully abandoned their practice of bypassing the question of what it is we value in tragedy by drawing arrows between statements in the *Poetics* and corresponding or nearly corresponding elements in works that we value. The *Poetics* became not so much a table of commandments as a sign of the covenant between literature and the ultimate values of the universe. The practical value that the Victorian and Edwardian critics found for Aristotle, and the one we have inherited from them, is suggested by the title S. H. Butcher gave to his translation of the *Poetics: Aristotle's Theory of Poetry and Fine Arts.* They insisted, in something like the manner of those of their schoolfellows who were biblical scholars, that what they possessed in the *Poetics* was, in Quiller-Couch's words, only "the fragment of a revised treatise"; but, like Butcher's title, they also insisted that there was a theory *there.*

The belief that there are about the *Poetics* the remains of a theory that defines tragedy once and for all has been a valuable tool in the criticism of the last hundred years. Aristotle's most popular phrases have been most popular as genies to be summoned when needed for occasional authority. Critics—particularly critics under pressure in classrooms—can leap to Aristotle when their own particular insights prove inconclusive. When a critic has said a number of true things about a dramatic tragedy and has not accounted for its grandeur or for whatever about it led him to put it in the special category *tragic,* he can give conclusion to his essay by saying that the qualities he has demonstrated in the play he discusses are qualities that evoke pity, fear, catharsis, or whatnot. Sudden, urgent, and imperfectly relevant Aristotelian endings to critical essays are only slightly more common than similar but humbler opening paragraphs in which the critic folds his particular arguments and insights into the universal by introducing them as handmaids to the evocation of pity and fear —handmaids whose duties are usually unspecified. Presumably everyone has read such essays and heard discussions of tragedy turned suddenly aside by a violent and unassailable appeal to the authority of pity and fear.

Any of that may be true, but none of it explains why a theory of tragedy should be more necessary to us than theories for other literary kinds. Why do we start from Aristotle instead of striking out into the field to make and report inductions? I suggest that tragedy is different from all the other things whose natures we want to know. Theories of the nature of tragedy are more important to us than theories of the nature of other things because theories of tragedy keep us from facing tragedy itself.

The last two sentences and particularly that cavalier "tragedy itself" need some explanation and justification. I pretty much have to try to say what tragedy is, and, with some humility, I will. Actually, however, that humility—though generally seemly—may be misplaced because what I mean to define now is not dramatic tragedy but real tragedy; in short, I mean to define the easier of the two, the one regularly and satisfactorily defined by critics—notably Hegel—who try to convince themselves that a definition of a tragic event can also serve as a definition of a tragic play.

So. What is tragedy? A word. What does that word do? It sets limits, fixes a category. What is in that category, "tragedy" (what *do* we put in it—not what *should* we put in it)? It is a category for things that should not have happened but can be neither remedied nor filed away under "things to have been expected under the given conditions."[1] It appears also, from observation of uses of the word *tragedy*, that its use is determined not so much by a particular quality of what happens as by a particular quality of our response to what happens—that tragedy is in the eye of the beholder. Whether or not we apply the word depends on whether or not at the moment of perception the norm violated by the tragic event has equal weight in our consciousness with the aberration that suddenly joins it there and can quickly supersede it as the working norm. In time of war, war becomes normal; in time of flood, flood does. We call wars tragic but rarely call the deaths of individual anonymous soldiers so; the same is true of floods, as opposed to particular drownings that occur during them. We use the word *tragedy* when we are confronted with a sudden invasion of our finite consciousness by the fact of infinite possibility—when our minds are sites for a domestic collision of the understanding and the fact of infinity. *Tragedy* is the word by which the mind designates (and thus in part denies) its helplessness before a concrete, particular, and thus undeniable demonstration of the limits of human understanding.

"Definition" (from *finis,* a limit, end), of tragedy is a contradiction in terms; and "tragedy," because it is a "term" (from *terminus,* a boundary, limit, end), denies the essence of what it labels: an experience of the fact of indefinition. The word *tragedy,* theories of tragedy (assisted by arguments about those theories and about what does or does not fit them), and the plays we call tragedies are—like this essay—benign (though futile) efforts to deny the existence of tragedy.

If what I have said about "real-life" tragedy is true, then a lot of critical practices about dramatic tragedy become understandable. If tragedy is a category for what cannot be categorized, the traditional expense of time and effort on defining dramatic tragedy is explicable as an extension of the emergency measure that the word *tragedy* is itself; the whole subject exists to cope with human nervousness at the fact of indefinition. One can see, too, why some people have wanted to devote themselves to checking particular plays against particulars of Aristotle's formulas. As long as they attempt mastery only of the obviously limited problem they present themselves, they can avoid facing the intellectual limitation of which tragedy is the terrible advertisement. Along with the clown in *Othello,* they can say, "To do this is within the compass of man's wit, and therefore I'll attempt the doing of it." Any theory of tragedy would do for such ceremonies of safety, but the complexity, the logical disjunction, and, above all, the vagueness of Aristotle's make it the only one sure to provide busywork for the mind sufficient to forestall the always threatening occasion for moving on to the tragic actualities of reading or seeing a dramatic tragedy.

One can understand also why it is in the interest of human comfort to insist that dramatic tragedy happens on the stage and not in the audience, where the only real action of a play must necessarily occur. Aristotle is not so insistent as most that the tragedy in a tragedy is of the characters—who think they understand something and do not —and not of the audience—who are there as understanders and do not understand. But the implications of Aristotle's doctrine of pity and fear seem to me to do an excellent job of letting us think that something less than tragedy occurs in the audience: what we can pity and fear is not happening to us. We may not end up with our heads on poles, but *Macbeth* puts us through an actual experience of the insufficiency of our finite minds to the infinite universe. What can be pitied and feared can be thought about, and, if after the play we can believe that we were pitying and fearing while it went on, then we have convinced ourselves that we are, were, and will remain in a knowable, limited universe.

A successful dramatic tragedy, as opposed to a play successful in fitting a critical formula, makes tragedy bearable; it lets us face truth beyond categories by presenting that unmanageable and undi-minished truth inside the irrationally comforting framework of the absolutely man-made, man-suited, and man-limited order of the play—the play as opposed to the materials and actions it describes or the experience of thinking about those materials and actions.

An audience may be able to face the existence of infinite possibility while the infinity of possibilities exercises itself within the humanly comprehensible confines of the play; but, when an audience thinks back on its experience of the events of the play, it feels the need to prove to itself that it could not have borne a demonstration of truth beyond reason. Enter criticism, therefore, often with the object of proving that indeed the audience has not borne and could not bear truth beyond reason, that there is no truth beyond reason, and that the success of the work of art—comprehending the incomprehensible in its artistic fabric—is not the action of the work of art but inherent in the nature of the materials. Aristotle's *Poetics* has been of invaluable assistance in that enterprise.

As I have already suggested, Aristotle's statements in the *Poetics,* like divinely revealed truth, have vatic sureness and authority as well as vatic vagueness and lack of fixed relation to one another. Pity and fear obviously have something to do with most things we call tragic, but what and how are not clear from Aristotle. The *Poetics* is more satisfying as an artistic inclusion of its troublesome subject matter than it is as an analysis. Aristotle keeps repeating his sensible-sounding assertions, and stringing them together with logical gestures we translate as *therefore*'s and *thus*'s; they sound truer and truer, and one becomes increasingly convinced that they really provide the definition of tragedy—which is to say, the limitation of tragedy —that they do not provide. Consider the most famous passage in the *Poetics;* this is the Butcher translation of the opening sentences of chapter 6:

> Of the poetry which imitates in hexameter verse, and of Comedy, we will speak hereafter. Let us now discuss Tragedy, resuming its formal definition, as resulting from what has been already said.
>
> Tragedy then, is an imitation of an action that is serious, complete, and of a certain magnitude; in language embellished with each kind of artistic ornament, the several kinds being found in separate parts of the play; in the form of action, not of narrative; through pity and fear effecting the proper purgation of these emotions. By "language embellished," I mean language into which rhythm, "harmony," and song enter. By "the several kinds in separate parts," I mean, that some parts are rendered through the medium of verse alone, others again with the aid of song.

In the Greek the passage makes its opening promise more explicitly than Butcher's version does. Aristotle says he will *pick the essential nature of tragedy out of what has been already said.* Most of what he says in the passage does indeed derive from and echo what has gone before, but "through pity and fear effecting the proper purgation of these emotions" is completely unprepared for, as well as imprecise and imprecisely related to its sentence. (Butcher's version is, if anything, clearer than the Greek, which says *by means of a course of events involving pity and fear, the purification of those painful fatal acts which have that quality.*) If one tries to figure out from the sentence just how pity and fear are used to purge pity and fear, or Aristotle's reasons for thinking that such purgation takes place, one is in trouble. But as one reads through the passage, one is not troubled. I suggest that here, as in the treatise at large, a primary value of the *Poetics* is not that it provides what we usually think of as a definition, but that it gives the things of tragedy definition—definition in the sense of giving them a local habitation. It satisfies because its readers feel the comforting confinement of limitations without knowing precisely *what* tragedy is limited *to*.

Whether the *Poetics* as we have it is or is not as Aristotle composed it, the *Poetics* as we have it is a superb container. The treatise keeps saying that it fits together logically. It actually fits together rhetorically, and does so largely by means of the persistent *sound* of logic. Aristotle says that dramatic tragedies need "an air of design" (9.11); "an air of design" is what the *Poetics* has. The passage I quoted before presents excellent examples in its elaborately formal establishment of a new heading and in its reassuringly logical use of *then* in "tragedy then is an imitation . . . ." Similarly, the sentences that follow the unexpected and unclear phrase about pity, fear, and purgation are sentences of painstaking explanation: just what are called for to give comfort and confidence to a reader. But look what is explained: "By 'language embellished,' I mean language into which rhythm, 'harmony,' and song enter. By the 'several kinds in separate parts,' I mean, that some parts are rendered through the medium of verse alone, others again with the aid of song." An explanation follows a need for explanation, but what is explained is *not* what needs explaining.

For another example, consider this paragraph (which occurs near the end of the chapter that starts with pity, fear, and purgation):

> The Plot, then, is the first principle, and, as it were, the soul of a tragedy: Character holds the second place. A similar fact is seen in painting. The most beautiful colors, laid on confusedly, will not give as much pleasure as the chalk outline of a portrait. Thus Tragedy is the imitation of an action, and of the agents mainly with a view to the action.

Although *then* in the first clause and *thus* in the last are excellent examples of logical gesture, I single out this paragraph because of a supralogic accidental to the painting analogy in the middle of the paragraph. The superiority of A to B—plot to character—is illustrated in the superiority of A' to B'—"the chalk outline of a portrait" to "beautiful colors, laid on confusedly." The same point could have been made with an alternate analogy like this one: "a similar fact is seen in music. The most beautiful tones, played randomly, will not give as much pleasure as a tune played on a pennywhistle."

The analogy in the *Poetics,* however, is much better than mine. For one thing, the painting analogy gets (and, since the modern phrase "colors of rhetoric" duplicates a Greek original, presumably always got) power and a feel of extra pertinence from the fact that "colors" —here used literally—relates metaphorically to the general topic to which the painting analogy is applied. More importantly, the painting analogy gets extra persuasiveness from the fact that the chalk-line portrait (A'), which in the logic of the analogy corresponds to plot (A), is—because of the substantive likeness between the verbal delineation of character and graphic delineation of a portrait— effectively synonymous with character (B), the element to which it contrasts. The argument for the primacy of plot over character thus comes wrapped in a nonlogical implication that the virtues of plot not only supersede but embody those of character.

As may by now be obvious, I am moving toward likening the *Poetics,* an action of artistic inclusion, to the dramatic tragedies it discusses. I said earlier that an audience thinking about a play in retrospect is unwilling to cast doubt on, or recognize its doubt about, its capacities for comprehension—as it would do if it attributed those temporary capacities to the enabling action of the work of art. An audience wants to believe that the comprehensibility given to tragic events by the comprehending—the encompassing—framework of the play is in the nature of the events themselves. That is to say that audiences—once they have seen or read a play—once they have become critics—attempt to maintain a belief, a belief engendered by the play and for its duration maintained by the play, that the comprehensibility of the container is of the nature of the thing contained. I suggest that at the heart of the whole matter of tragedy is a desirable confusion between the events we call tragic and the plays we call tragic, between real tragedy and dramatic tragedy. That confusion, I think, is fundamental to the success of Aristotle's *Poetics* as a work of art.

The *Poetics* blurs the distinction between the events depicted in dramatic tragedy and an audience's experience of that depiction. In many of its most popular particulars the *Poetics* tends to confirm the desired impression that the events described in dramatic tragedies are of themselves as intellectually manageable as they become inside the artistic framework provided by the play. Throughout the *Poetics* there is regular confusion between what Aristotle requires of the *play* and what he requires of the actions described *in* the play. He says, for example, that he is concerned with the *structure of* tragedies (what he calls plot), but most of his demands concern the actions *described in* tragedies (what we call plot). He persistently asks that the people and events of the story be such as to do much of the play's work for it; he asks that what goes on in the play conform to (and thus confirm the sufficiency of) the range of possibilities determined by the limited range of human understanding.

Some of the best loved of Aristotle's dicta on the kinds of events properly described in dramatic tragedy seem to bar those that we are most likely to call tragic in real life and some of those described in the examples Aristotle works from: "The poet should prefer probable impossibilities to improbable possibilities. The tragic plot must not be composed of irrational parts. Everything irrational should, if possible, be excluded" (24.10). Tragedies do not exclude the irrational; they *in*clude it; Aristotle's favorite model, *Oedipus Rex,* is proof against him. His principal demands for the events of tragedy are of two general but related kinds: he asks for, and insists that he finds, unity and rationality. Both of those are foreign to what I take to be the essence of the events we label "tragedy." Unity fills the same psychological need filled by the closed categories that tragedy explodes; a unified action is finite, limited, just as Aristotle says it is. As for rationality, by seeking a cause for every effect in tragedies, Aristotle denied that there is tragedy, that things happen to people and that people do things that will not fit our capacity to understand them. With the theory of the tragic flaw, he asserts the limitless validity of the most comforting of human ideas: error. Aristotle's demands for rational limits to the events in a dramatic tragedy can all be seen as extensions from the play to its story of his just demand that a play have "a beginning, a middle, and an end"—in short that it have definition, limits.

It is easy enough to see that in the tragedies we value, the *imitation* (the play) is complete, has a beginning, a middle, and an end. That is not often true of the actions imitated; it is notably untrue in *Macbeth.*

It is true that *Macbeth* very definitely begins—more definitely than *King Lear* or *Othello* or *Hamlet,* which open on continuing situations. In *Macbeth* the witches come out and plan future action ("When shall we three meet again?") and promise an immediate relationship to the title character ("There to meet with Macbeth" —I.i.7). *Macbeth* also ends. Macduff enters with the head of Mac-

beth; everyone hails Malcolm king, and, in the last speech of the play,
Malcolm ties off all the loose threads of Scottish politics:

> We shall not spend a large expense of time
> Before we reckon with your several loves
> And make us even with you. My Thanes and kinsmen,
> Henceforth be Earls, the first that ever Scotland
> In such an honor named. What's more to do
> Which would be planted newly with the time—
> As calling home our exiled friends abroad
> That fled the snares of watchful tyranny,
> Producing forth the cruel ministers
> Of this dead butcher and his fiend-like queen,
> Who (as 'tis thought) by self and violent hands
> Took off her life—this, and what needful else
> That calls upon us, by the grace of Grace
> We will perform in measure, time, and place.
> So thanks to all at once and to each one,
> Whom we invite to see us crowned at Scone.

On the other hand, it would also be true to say that *Macbeth* is all
middle. For instance, this eminently final speech of Malcolm's is
curiously reminiscent of Duncan's speeches when the earlier hurly-
burly was done, when the earlier battle was lost and won. In Act
I—with Macdonwald's head newly fixed upon the battlements in the
midst of a battle that seems done and then picks up again—Duncan
promised rewards and distributed titles. Specifically, Malcolm's distribution of earldoms and his general invitation to ceremonial jour-
neying echo Duncan's gestures in I.iv.35—43:

> Sons, kinsmen, thanes,
> And you whose places are the nearest, know
> We will establish our estate upon
> Our eldest, Malcolm, whom we name hereafter
> The Prince of Cumberland; which honor must
> Not unaccompanied invest him only,
> But signs of nobleness, like stars, shall shine
> On all deservers. From hence to Inverness,
> And bind us further to you.

Malcolm's "What's more to do / Which would be planted newly with
the time" echoes Duncan's metaphor when he addresses Macbeth at
their first (and only) onstage meeting: "I have begun to plant thee and

will labor / To make thee full of growing." A vague, free-floating sense that the old cycle is starting over again in the new can also be evoked by the deluge of *Hail*'s that greets Malcolm's reign, as the witches hailed Macbeth's. Moreover, Malcolm's speech also denies its finality by introducing an audience that is six lines from the end of the play to new and doubtful information about Lady Macbeth, who has, for the last three scenes, been dead and done with in the audience's understanding.

The inconclusiveness coeval with the close of the action and the end of the play is—to the dismay of generations of actors and critics— actually demonstrated on the stage.

Macbeth speaks his last line, "Lay on, Macduff, / And damned be him that first cries, 'Hold, enough!' " (V.viii.33−34). The sentence asserts continuation. But its occasion bespeaks finality: Macbeth is trying "the last"; this is a fight to the death. The couplet rhyme bespeaks finality too. The immediately ensuing action is simultaneously complete (*Exeunt*—the scene is over) and incomplete (Macbeth and Macduff go off fighting, and we hear the fight continuing offstage). Then the completed scene continues. Macduff drives Macbeth right back out on the stage again and kills him.

Macbeth has no death speech, and the traditional wonder at that fact derives, I think, not so much from our sympathy with actor-managers deprived of a professional perquisite, as from a general theatrical awkwardness—an awkwardness inconsistent with our need for, and expectations of, theatrical and narrative finality, but an awkwardness entirely consistent with the behavior of this play. When a character is fatally injured in a sword fight, his corpse lies on the stage breathing heavily; if the winded actor has a death speech to say—a speech in which he announces that he now is dead, he now is fled, and his soul is in the sky, then the undoubted expiration of the character and the obvious respiration of the actor are isolated from one another, each in its proper category within the double experience of the audience, which always sees two things at once: actors on a stage and characters in a story. After Macbeth speaks what turns out to be his last line, the Folio stage direction say, *Exeunt fighting. Alarums. Enter Fighting, and Macbeth slaine.* The action called for by those directions tells an audience that Macbeth is dead—if only because there is no more plot left to be worked out. But the audience's knowledge is not neat, does not have comfortable handles on it, because Macbeth is not labeled as dead. The audience must itself maintain the equilibrium between the two realities while Macduff (or his director) manages to get the puffing corpse of Macbeth off the stage.

I have talked enough about the last moments of Macbeth the character and the last moments of *Macbeth* the play. By way of coda, however, let me point out that the nineteen-line interval between *Enter Fighting, and Macbeth slaine* and *Enter Macduffe; with Macbeths head* is largely taken up with an ostentatiously precise discussion of the state, location, and proper response to another corpse, that of young Siward:

> *Ross.* Your son, my lord, has paid a soldier's debt.
>   He only lived but till he was a man,
>   The which no sooner had his prowess confirmed
>   In the unshrinking station where he fought
>   But like a man he died.
> *Siward.*   Then he is dead?
> *Ross.* Ay, and brought off the field. Your cause of sorrow
>   Must not be measured by his worth, for then
>   It hath no end.
> *Siward.*   Had he his hurts before?
> *Ross.* Ay, on the front.
> *Siward.*   Why then, God's soldier be he.
>   [V.viii.39–47]

The dead Macbeth "hath no end"—at least no theatrically comfortable end. On the other hand, young Siward, who never strikes us as more than an incidental of the play, is put to rest with full expository rites. This displaced fulfillment of the audience's need for certainty operates comparably to the similar displacement in the *Poetics* when "language embellished" is defined instead of "pity," "fear" and "purgation."

Finality is regularly unattainable throughout *Macbeth:* Macbeth and Lady Macbeth cannot get the murder of Duncan finished: Lady Macbeth has to go back with the knives. They cannot get done with Duncan himself: his blood will not wash off. Banquo refuses death in two ways: he comes back as a ghost, and (supposedly) he lives on in the line of Stuart kings into the actual present of the audience. The desirability and impossibility of conclusion is a regular concern of the characters, both in large matters ("The time has been / That, when the brains were out, the man would die, / And there an end" —III.iv.78−80) and in such smaller ones as Macbeth's inability to achieve the temporary finality of sleep and Lady Macbeth's inability to cease her activity even in sleep itself. The concern for finality is incidentally present even in details like Macbeth's incapacity to pronounce "Amen."

What is true of endings is also true of beginnings. Lady Macbeth's mysteriously missing children present an ominous, unknown, but undeniable time before the beginning. Doubtful beginnings are also incidentally inherent in such details of the play as Macduff's nonbirth. Indeed, the beginnings, sources, causes, of almost everything in the play are at best nebulous.

Cause and effect do not work in *Macbeth.* The play keeps giving the impression that Lady Macbeth is the source of ideas and the instigator of actions that are already underway. For example, in III.ii the audience may have an impression that Lady Macbeth has some responsibility for the coming attack on Banquo and Fleance, but Macbeth has already commissioned the murderers. People have also tried to show that Lady Macbeth is as much the source of the idea of murdering Duncan as she seems to be. In fact, it is almost impossible to find the source of any idea in *Macbeth;* every new idea seems already there when it is presented to us. The idea of regicide really originates in the mind of the audience, which comes into a world that presents only the positive action of treason or the negative action of opposing it.

The play, as play, has definition—a beginning, a middle, and an end—but its materials, even those that are used to designate its limits, provide insistent testimony to the artificiality, frailty, and ultimate impossibility of limits. A sense of limitlessness infuses every element of the play.

A good short example is the operation of limitless and directionless time in Macbeth's speech on the death of Lady Macbeth:

> She should have died hereafter:
> There would have been a time for such a word.
> To-morrow, and to-morrow, and to-morrow
> Creeps in this petty pace from day to day
> To the last syllable of recorded time,

And all our yesterdays have lighted fools
The way to dusty death. Out, out, brief candle!
Life's but a walking shadow, a poor player
That struts and frets his hour upon the stage
And then is heard no more. It is a tale
Told by an idiot, full of sound and fury,
Signifying nothing.

[V.v.17−28]

"Hereafter," which designates time future, here echoes time past in the play. It echoes Lady Macbeth's first words to Macbeth. In their first exchange, "by the all-hail hereafter" itself is an echo of the witches' prophecy of Macbeth's future ("All hail, Macbeth! that shalt be King hereafter"—I.iii.50), and it leads first into her lines on her sense of the future (even as she, who was not present when the witches spoke, is displaying knowledge of the past that she does not have) and then into a forecast of the immediate future, from which her death results and which is figured as a tomorrow that will never come:

Great Glamis! worthy Cawdor!
Greater than both, by the all-hail hereafter!
Thy letters have transported me beyond
This ignorant present, and I feel now
The future in the instant.
Macbeth.   My dearest love
Duncan comes here to-night.
Lady.   And when goes hence?
Macbeth. To-morrow, as he purposes.
Lady,   O, never
Shall sun that morrow see!

[I.v.52−59]

Tomorrow designates time future, but in the construction "Tomorrow, and tomorrow, and tomorrow" its plurality suggests its operation in the past, while the tense of the verb, *creeps,* is present. The direction in which it creeps should be future, but the ultimate future is described in words ("last," "recorded") that suit and suggest the ultimate past. The next clause is actually in the past tense. The journey of yesterdays becomes undistinguishable from that of tomorrows, and time past fuses with time future. "Out, out," the candle, and the walking shadow in the next lines suggest Lady Macbeth in the sleepwalking scene and thus, in a sense, introduce her alive into a speech of which her death is the occasion but of which she seemed no longer to be the subject.

Nothing in the play or in the speech is finished for good. Look at the way the general subject introduced by the use of the word *word* to mean "message" in line 18 and established in the reiteration of the word *tomorrow* reappears unexpectedly in *syllable, heard,* and *told.* Even the metaphors for the transitory life of man are of a piece with the play: "a walking shadow"—ghosts are notorious for perseverance—and "a poor player"—actors whose parts run out return in another character (in fact, the actor who played Lady Macbeth might already have returned as one or more servants or messengers).

In *Macbeth* no kind of closed category will stay closed around any object. The validity of that general assertion can be demonstrated in the details of almost any scene in the play. I will, however, concentrate on the second scene, the scene that gives an audience its first solid information about the situation from which the play will unfold, and a scene in which characters perform similar but more limited services for other characters. In scene ii, the categories *good* and *bad* fail: Macbeth and Banquo are lumped together, and are in turn hard to distinguish from the traitors. The Captain's first speech provides a good example both of the behavior of the scene and of the play; its first line describes the phenomenon I am talking about: "Doubtful it stood."

> Doubtful it stood,
> As two spent swimmers that do cling together
> And choke their art. The merciless Macdonwald
> (Worthy to be a rebel, for to that
> The multiplying villainies of nature
> Do swarm upon him) from the Western Isles
> Of kerns and gallowglasses is supplied;
> And Fortune, on his damned quarrel smiling,
> Showed like a rebel's whore. But all's too weak:
> For brave Macbeth (well he deserves that name),
> Disdaining Fortune, with his brandished steel,
> Which smoked with bloody execution,
> Like valor's minion carved out his passage
> Till he faced the slave;
> Which ne'er shook hands nor bade farewell to him

Till he unseamed him from the nave to th' chops
And fixed his head upon our battlements.

[I.ii.7 − 23]

Not only does the speech describe the forces of good and evil so intertwined as to be indistinguishable, it goes on to describe the fight between the evil Macdonwald and the good Macbeth in such a way as to make Macbeth deserving of the epithet applied to Macdonwald—"merciless." Macdonwald is called evil, and Macbeth good, but they are described in a pair of roughly parallel sentences in which they are to some extent equated by echoes—"merciless Macdonwald / (Worthy to be a rebel . . .)" is balanced by "brave Macbeth (well he deserves that name)." Moreover—partly because Macdonwald is described only in passive constructions and partly because Macbeth is so impersonal, ruthless, and violent—Macbeth, the defender of right, sounds more a monster of cruelty than Macdonwald does.

Throughout the Captain's narrative, the doers of good sound either like or worse than the evildoers. Sentences like the one that caps his report of the valor of Macbeth and Banquo by suggesting that they "meant to . . . memorize another Golgotha" (I.ii.39 − 40), are stylistic analogues to the perverse meterological commonplace the Captain gratuitously introduces as prelude to his account of the Norwegian attack:

As whence the sun 'gins his reflection
Shipwracking storms and direful thunders break,
So from that spring whence comfort seemed to come
Discomfort swells.

[I.ii.25 − 28]

Later in the scene—but in a grosser dimension—the category "Cawdor" (a traitor's title bestowed upon the leader of the loyal force that defeated the traitor), becomes as inefficient in its designation as "brave Macbeth" became in the Captain's first speech. As the play progresses, Macbeth and Lady Macbeth are often hard to distinguish, and they are like several other characters who are regularly in doubt about their own and other people's sexes. Categories will not define. Words, notably the word *man,* whose meaning characters periodically worry over, will not define. The most obvious examples of the insufficiency of limits are the equivocations that are one of the play's recurrent topics. In an equivocation—as in a pun—one is presented with a situation in which sentences and words, things that exist only to define, do not define, do not set limits. One could say, in fact, that *Macbeth* is itself, as a whole, a kind of equivocation between the fact of limitlessness—indefinition, tragedy—and the duty of art to limit and define.

The varieties of incidentally indefinite acts of incidental verbal definition in scene ii are dizzyingly numerous. Consider, for instance, the Captain's response to Duncan's "Dismayed not this / Our captains, Macbeth and Banquo?" (I.ii.33−34). The Captain's answer is "Yes"; but his next line turns yes to no: "As sparrows eagles, or the hare the lion." Also consider the later, altogether surmountable but nonetheless real, doubt about the references of names, epithets, and pronouns that not quite obviously refer to the King of Norway in Ross's report of the battle. His first reference, to "Norway himself" (51), is transparently clear, but—when, eight lines later, Ross calls the king by name—the mere fact of the addition and the fact that the specific name is introduced late and after it is useful in identifying its bearer make the action precisely counterproductive as an act of identification and cause a confusion that Ross parenthetically combats as soon as he speaks the name: "Sweno, the Norways' king, craves composition" (59). In the lines that intervene between the identification of the King as "Norway himself" and his identification as "Sweno," he is the logically demonstrable syntactic referent for "him" in the lines where Ross describes the combat between "Bellona's bridegroom" and "him":

> Norway himself, with terrible numbers,
> Assisted by that most disloyal traitor
> The Thane of Cawdor, began a dismal conflict,
> Till that Bellona's bridegroom, lapped in proof,
> Confronted him with self-comparisons,
> Point against point rebellious, arm 'gainst arm,
> Curbing his lavish spirit . . .
>
> [51−57]

Although *Assisted by that most disloyal traitor / The Thane of Cawdor* is, like *with terrible numbers,* merely parenthetical, a modifier (or a modifier for a modifier) for *Norway himself,* these lines can easily seem to describe a confrontation not between Macbeth and the Norwegian king but between Macbeth and Cawdor. That is so because the name *Cawdor* is physically nearer to the pronoun *him* than *Norway* is, and because the lines particularize Cawdor ("that most disloyal traitor") and thus present him to a hearer's imagination as confrontable—as a more easily imagined party to a hand-to-hand combat than Norway is—and because, although a tributary king who invades his superior's territory can be considered a traitor, Cawdor—a Scot and Duncan's thane—more obviously fits the label *traitor* than Norway does.[2]

For a very different sort of indefinite act of verbal definition, consider "Which ne'er shook hands nor bade farewell" (I.ii. 21—in the speech of the wounded Captain that I quoted earlier, the one that begins "Doubtful it stood"). The line embodies a purely incidental instance of non-beginning and non-ending. Since a handshake is as appropriate to greeting as to parting, the line embodies one more substantially gratuitous dubiety in the fact that "bade farewell" pairs with "shook hands" either as its complementary opposite or as a redundant synonym added for emphasis. Moreover, the bluff, soldierly irony of using gestures of friendly meeting as metaphors for hand-to-hand combat presents a casual stylistic echo of the confusion of opposites that characterizes the speech at large.

In fact, the large action of that speech is itself doubtful. At the point when the opening assertion is made, "Doubtful it stood" reports "the newest state" "of the revolt" (2–3); the antecedent for *it* is *the broil* in the instruction to which the Captain responds, "Say to the King the knowledge of the broil / As thou didst leave it" (6–7). The Captain's plural simile—the "two spent swimmers that do cling together" (and who, thus intertwined, become an entity in which the two independent beings are indistinguishable)—describes the same singular antecedent: the broil. However, in the lines that follow, the two swimmers, because they *are* two, come to function like emblems for the two men to whom the Captain's account next proceeds: "merciless Macdonwald" and "brave Macbeth," adversaries whose defining qualities become as confused as the bodies of the two intertwined swimmers in the simile (a simile that described not the two principals in the broil but the broil itself), and adversaries whose defining qualities only become confused as a direct result of the Captain's adjectival insistence on the distinction between the merciless villain and Macbeth.

Similarly, but in another dimension, this speech that began by saying that, at the time the Captain left the field, the state of the broil was doubtful concludes with a substantively and rhythmically conclusive report on the demise of the rebel leader. The speech's last two lines conclude an account that has changed its identity in passage. They conclude a speech quite different from the speech this one set out to be. The newly emergent speech is one that says, "At one point the outcome of the battle was in doubt; then Macbeth attacked Macdonwald and overcame him." However, neither our new understanding of the logical function of the phrase "Doubtful it stood" nor the finality implied by Macdonwald's defeat persists.

Immediately after the speech has—in "And fixed his head upon our battlements"—announced exactly the sort of fixed conclusion to the broil that its first words had at first said was unavailable, the cycle resumes. No sooner has Duncan expressed his pleasure and relief than (with typically and appropriately perverse indirection of syntax and substance) the Captain continues his account to say that, after the defeat of Macdonwald, the battle unexpectedly revived. The Captain thus revives the validity of his opening assertion that the outcome of the battle was undetermined when he left it:

> . . . he unseamed him from the nave to th' chops
> And fixed his head upon our battlements.
> *King.* O valiant cousin! worthy gentleman!
> *Captain.* As whence the sun 'gins his reflection
> Shipwracking storms and direful thunders break,
> So from that spring whence comfort seemed to come
> Discomfort swells. Mark, King of Scotland, mark.
> No sooner justice had, with valor armed,
> Compelled these skipping kerns to trust their heels
> But the Norweyan lord, surveying vantage,
> With furbished arms and new supplies of men,
> Began a fresh assault.

[I.ii.22–33]

As the Captain's first conclusive speech proved to be inconclusive, and as the news he brought is, by his own opening assertion, inconclusive, so—too weak to continue—he breaks off in mid-sentence and retires. He is immediately succeeded by a new arrival, Ross, who brings fresh and final news. The finality of Ross's news, however, is itself shaky. His first speech ends with "and to conclude, / The vic-

tory fell on us." "Great happiness!" says Duncan. And, though the
reported victory does indeed turn out to be conclusive, Ross continues his apparently complete sentence—continues it with fresh news
about the Norwegian king, who had been the cause that the earlier
account, the Captain's account of Macdonwald's defeat, had needed
continuation:

> . . . and to conclude,
> The victory fell on us.
> *King.*　　　　　　Great happiness!
> *Ross.*　　　　　　　　　　That now
> Sweno, the Norways' king, craves composition;
> Nor would we deign him burial of his men
> Till he disbursed, at Saint Colme's Inch,
> Ten thousand dollars to our general use.
>
> 　　　　　　　　　　　　　　　[I.ii.57–62]

This time the additional news is merely confirmatory, and the scene
ends. But it ends with a promise of continuation of another sort:
Duncan sends Ross to bestow Cawdor's title on Macbeth.

What is true of words, sentences, and speeches is also true of the
characters in *Macbeth;* they will not stay within limits either. Take,
for example, the witches—the first characters we apprehend and the
first characters the play tells us we comprehend. They intend to
"meet with Macbeth." Are they his accomplices or his enemies? The
play behaves as if that were immediately obvious to us, but it is not.
We are also ignorant of their relation to the action: do they foresee
events or ordain them? Banquo encapsulates the issue and —in the
manner by which the whole play takes us through and beyond the
doubts it contains—overwhelms the problem in a syntax that casually
fuses the alternatives:

> If you can look into the seeds of time
> And say which grain will grow and which will not,
> Speak then to me, who neither beg nor fear
> Your favors nor your hate.
>
> 　　　　　　　　　　　　　　　[I.iii.58–63]

Among the many other things we do not finally know is whether
the witches are natural or supernatural. If natural, are they male or are
they female? The actors Shakespeare's audience saw were male, but
what about the three bearded sisters those men played? They are

indisputably female, but the play insists that we momentarily pursue the issue before returning to the facts already obvious from the repetition of the word *sister* and manifest in the pronoun *her* even at the moment of gratuitous, theatrically complicated doubt:

> You seem to understand me,
> By each at once her choppy finger laying
> Upon her skinny lips. You should be women,
> And yet your beards forbid me to interpret
> That you are so.

[I.iii.43−47]

And, if the witches are not natural, are they real or imaginary? Where in the spectrum of unnatural evidences do they belong? We are asked to think of the dagger Macbeth sees in II.i as "a dagger of the mind"; after their last appearance we have a chance to think similarly of the witches: they should have passed Lennox, but Lennox did not see them (IV.i.136−37). They could be like Banquo's ghost—apparently not imaginary but visible only to Macbeth. But Banquo saw the witches on the heath in I.iii (when they arrived "there to meet with Macbeth" and met with and prophesied to both Macbeth and Banquo). Moreover, and most important, they are the first characters we see and are therefore in a way "realer" to us than anyone else in the subsequent fiction. At any given moment our minds must and do behave as if they knew the nature of the witches, but in retrospect we do not know.

What matters here is not hunting down an answer to the question "What are the witches?" All the critical and theatrical efforts to answer that question demonstrate that the question cannot be answered. What those frantic answers also demonstrate—and what matters—is the fact of the question. The play does not require that it be answered. Thinking about the play's action does. As we watch the play, the witches have definition, but we cannot afterward say what that definition is. As we watch the play, we know what we cannot know; we possess knowledge that remains unattainable. That kind of paradoxical capacity is, I think, what the play gives us that makes us call it great.

The greatness of *Macbeth*, I think, derives from Shakespeare's ability to minimize neither our sense of limitlessness nor our sense of the constant and comforting limitation of artistic pattern, order, and coherence. Macbeth's soliloquy at the beginning of I.vii provides a microcosm of the whole—a microcosm in which Shakespeare's double action is well demonstrated and which contains examples of most of the qualities I have described.

The soliloquy is the first event of the night of the murder of Duncan—a night that is made to seem endless on the stage, and one that will not end in the play: it is replayed in the sleepwalking scene. The speech is concerned in a variety of ways with conclusion—with being done. The speech itself does not conclude, but is broken off by the entrance of Lady Macbeth, who comes to say that Duncan has almost finished dinner and to inform Macbeth that the event he has been deliberating is already under way:

> If it were done when 'tis done, then 'twere well
> It were done quickly. If th' assassination
> Could trammel up the consequence, and catch
> With his surcease success, that but this blow
> Might be the be-all and the end-all—; here,
> But here upon this bank and shoal of time,
> We'ld jump the life to come. But in these cases
> We still have judgment here, that we but teach
> Bloody instructions, which, being taught, return
> To plague th' inventor. This even-handed justice
> Commends th' ingredience of our poisoned chalice
> To our own lips. He's here in double trust:
> First, as I am his kinsman and his subject,
> Strong both against the deed; then, as his host,
> Who should against his murderer shut the door,
> Not bear the knife myself. Besides, this Duncan
> Hath borne his faculties so meek, hath been
> So clear in his great office, that his virtues
> Will plead like angels, trumpet-tongued against
> The deep damnation of his taking-off;
> And pity, like a naked new-born babe
> Striding the blast, or heaven's cherubin horsed
> Upon the sightless couriers of the air,
> Shall blow the horrid deed in every eye
> That tears shall drown the wind. I have no spur
> To prick the sides of my intent, but only

Vaulting ambition, which o'erleaps itself
And falls on th' other—
    Enter Lady Macbeth.
                    How now? What news?
                                    [I.vii.1—28]

Nothing here will stay fixed. We would stand here *and* jump there.[3] Time and place will not stay fixed. Even the meaning of the word *but* (lines 4, 6, 7, 8, 26) will not stay fixed. And notice, in lines 12—16, how the two of "double trust" turns out to be three: "I am his kinsman and his subject . . . [and] his host." The process by which pairs turn into trios in this baby-ridden play is at its largest in III.iii, when the third murderer inexplicably presents himself to the other two.[4] In the last sentence of the soliloquy the sequence of images is peculiarly appropriate both to this play—in which beginning, end, first, and last are nearly meaningless concepts—and to the sentence itself—which describes failure and fails to conclude: the metaphor of spurring (done in the saddle), *precedes* the metaphor of mounting. The speech destroys the idea that any action can be finished; it makes the very idea of limits ridiculous. The word *success* in "catch with his surcease, success" is emblematic of the speech and the play. *Success* suggests both triumphant final achievement and, as its Latin root indicates, "that which follows," "succession."

The speech is terrifyingly limitless, but at the same time it is, like the play, ordered, unified, and coherent. Like the coherences by which the whole play is given order, identity, and thus definition, the elements that order the speech are simultaneously those that evoke our sense of its intellectually unmanageable vastness. The word *success,* for example, participates in the ostentatiously artificial aural harmony of "surcease, success." And, although the word *but* changes its meaning randomly, its very repetition gives lines 4—8 a nonlogical sound of order and regularity. Similarly the word *blow,* which in lines 4 and 24 is used in two generally contradictory senses in two generally contradictory sentences, gives the speech some coherence —some identity—by the mere fact of its repetition. The complex nonlogical interrelation among the polyptoton in "bear" and "borne," the pun on "bear the knife" and "bare the knife," and "naked [bare] new-*born* babe" has a similar effect. So has the equestrian metaphorical common denominator of the "cherubin horsed" and "vaulting ambition" in the last two sentences. So, too, have the link between the metaphysical "jump" in line 7 and the leaping in the last two lines and the drift that occurs between "striding"—walking across —"the blast" and its immediate successor, the idea of riding a horse, *be*striding a horse.

The double action of dramatic tragedy in general, of *Macbeth,* and of this speech in particular is summed up in the phrase "pity, like a naked new-born babe / Striding the blast." The phrase is vivid, particular, and intensely visual; *and*—if only because our memories of newborn babies cannot adapt to our mental picture of a striding human figure—cannot be visualized (if you doubt me, just try in your mind's eye to *see* the personified "pity" the phrase assures you it has empowered you to imagine). The phrase is wonderful in all that word's pertinent senses: it is superb; it is amazing; and it is a container filled by a marvel unlimited and undiminished by encapsulation. The phrase presents something limitless—beyond human comprehension—presents it in limited, comprehensible terms and leaves it still the limitless, incomprehensible, unimaginable thing it is.

2. *Fair is Foul, and Foul is Fair*

I submit that the tragedy of the play *Macbeth* is not of the character Macbeth and that it does not happen on the stage. The tragedy occurs in the audience, in miniature in each little failure of categories and at its largest in the failure of active moral categories to hold the actions and actors proper to them. An audience undergoes its greatest tragedy in joining its mind to Macbeth's both in his sensitive awareness of evil and his practice of it. Like Macbeth, it knows evil but, even in the last two acts when Malcolm is repeatedly proferred as the wholesome substitute for Macbeth, it persists in seeing the play through Macbeth's eyes. The audience itself cannot keep itself in the category dictated by its own morality, even though its moral judgments of characters and their actions are dictated entirely by that morality.

There is an obvious but inadequate reason why our sympathy with Macbeth has the intensity implied by that word's etymological roots in Greek words for "together" and "to experience" ("to feel," "to suffer," "to undergo"): we see things from Macbeth's point of view—in the metaphoric sense of *see*—because, for most of the play's length, Macbeth is in fact the principal conduit through which we are informed of events and their progress. The same, however, is true of Richard in *Richard III* and Iago in *Othello;* audiences' relations with them are close (and disturbing to think about after the fact), but, where we never lose our identities as observers of Richard and Iago, to be audience to *Macbeth* is virtually to *be* Macbeth for the duration of the performance. (That that is so is demonstrated by the fact that it has occurred to so many commentators to deny it—to argue that we do not identify ourselves with Macbeth as they would never bother to argue—or imagine a need to argue—that we do not identify ourselves with Richard or Iago.)

The reason for the morally improbable spiritual fusion between the virtuous and high-minded audience and the wicked, morally shallow Macbeth is, I think, that—until Lady Macbeth's sleepwalking scene (V.i)—Macbeth and the audience are (with the possible and fascinatingly perverse exception of the comically philosophical Porter) the only major parties to the play who see or feel the magnitude of the situations and events the play presents. Although Macbeth's superbly vivid imagination reaches no further than "stick-and-carrot" moral economics,[5] Macbeth is the only character in the play who is our size.

Even the witches behave as if Macbeth, his crimes, and his fortune were on the same scale with those of the tempest-tossed sailor "to Aleppo gone, master o' th' Tiger" (I.iii.7). And the events of the play never evoke more from Banquo than gentlemanly musings. Duncan sounds hardly more than bemused at Cawdor's treachery; he immediately resumes his complacent confidence in social order. Banquo and Duncan sum up their radical blandness in their slow, luxuriously fatuous commentary on the salubrious climate at Macbeth's castle (I.vi.1–10). As to Lady Macbeth—waking, she treats any challenge as a limited problem in logistics. Macduff, who responds passionately, if unimaginatively, to Duncan's murder, is thereafter principally noteworthy for absenting himself from one place or another. In IV.iii, the "England" scene where he hears and responds to the news that his wife and children have been slaughtered, Macduff has and takes his one opportunity to command the full attention of the audience. But, even then, that generally debilitating scene is contrived in such a way as to emphasize Macduff's passivity and impotence.

It is, however, Malcolm whom IV.iii treats most harshly.

Having mentioned IV.iii, the only slow scene in the play, and come to Malcolm in my list of characters whose scale of response is inferior to Macbeth's and the audience's, I want to pause and look at both that scene and Malcolm in detail. Together they provide means for more fully developing the idea of the audience's tragic loss of its comfortable confidence in the limits of its own potential.

Early in the play—in his forthright, personal greeting to the bloody sergeant who earlier had helped him in battle (I.ii.3—5) and in the large-mindedness of his account of Cawdor's death (I.iv.3—11) —Malcolm shows signs of just the sort of spiritual energy he would need if he were to separate the audience's soul from Macbeth's. Malcolm does not speak again, however, until after his father's murder:

Macduff. Your royal father's murdered.
Malcolm.   O, by whom?

                                                                    [II.iii.96]

I have yet to hear an actor sufficient to overcome the inherent silliness of "O, by whom?"—a response from which no amount of gasping and mimed horror can remove the tone of small talk.

Malcolm speaks twice more before he and Donalbain are left alone onstage to close II.iii with their plans for flight. After "O, by whom?" his next speech (II.iii.115—16), is an all-but-overt comment on Shakespeare's tactic in rendering our potential hero theatrically impotent: "Why do we hold our tongues, / That most may claim this argument for ours?" Donalbain's answer, though its substance is hardly heroic, is vigorously phrased. Malcolm contents himself with tacking a final phrase (II.iii.120—21) to Donalbain's syntax—or, rather, Shakespeare contents *him*self with making Malcolm weak, not just weak in terms of the dramatized situation but, unlike Donalbain, theatrically weak: Shakespeare makes Malcom a role in which no actor has a chance of capturing our attention. Malcolm does not appear again until IV.iii—where Shakespeare entirely undoes him by making his presence painful to his moral allies, the audience.

Malcolm's behavior in IV.iii is the most perverse element in a perverse scene. Malcolm is obviously perverse in vilifying himself to test Macduff's political idealism, but the perversity that concerns me here is not so much of the character as of the characterization. An irritating character—one who irritates his fellow characters as Polonius, Hotspur, and Juliet's Nurse do—is neither necessarily nor usually irritating to an audience. Shakespeare, however, makes the honorable, purposeful Malcom a theatrical irritation. His first lengthy speech in the scene (lines 8−17: "What I believe, I'll wail; / What know, believe; and what I can redress, / As I shall find the time to friend, I will . . ."), is not only bombastic in substance but bombasted out with syntactical stuffing (like "As I shall find the time to friend," which keeps a generally hollow sentence from reaching its hollow close).

As the speech progresses—and in the speeches that continue from it (lines 18−24, 25−31)—Malcolm's style is grating in its lack of economy: he both offers us luxurious appositives for phrases that need no clarification and uses elliptically foreshortened constructions that save time at the expense of an audience's ease of understanding (consider, for example, "and wisdom," a particularly crabbed ellipsis for "and it may be wise," in "and wisdom / To offer up a weak, poor, innocent lamb" [lines 15−16]). Then, when he comes to self-slander (which, though odd, could have been interesting to listen to), Malcolm's syntax is maddeningly contorted, and his pace tortuous. For instance, he spends several slow, unnecessary lines making it difficult for Macduff and the audience to be entirely certain they know who it is he is talking about:

> But, for all this,
> When I shall tread upon the tyrant's head
> Or wear it on my sword, yet my poor country
> Shall have more vices than it had before,
> More suffer, and more sundry ways than ever,
> By him that shall succeed.
> *Macduff.*   What should he be?
> *Malcolm.* It is myself I mean . . .
>
> [IV.iii.44−50]

Malcolm thereupon invites Macduff to debate his claim to villainy greater than Macbeth's. Malcolm's response to Macduff's case for Macbeth's superior villainy piles specifics on for emphasis and thereby delays the progress of the scene; no quantity of alternative adjectives and nouns can fill up the cistern of Malcolm's lust to dilate upon particulars:

> I grant him bloody,
> Luxurious, avaricious, false, deceitful,

Sudden, malicious, smacking of every sin
That has a name. But there's no bottom, none,
In my voluptuousness. Your wives, your daughters,
Your matrons, and your maids could not fill up
The cistern of my lust . . .

[57−63]

Detailed demonstration of Malcolm's syntactic perversity and the lack of expository economy in the several speeches by which he finally exhausts Macduff's patience and prepares the way for the speech (114−37) in which he ponderously takes back all he has said against himself would be as tedious as the scene is. That is less true of the scene's more obviously frustrating second movement.

Ross, who enters a scene that has been previously concerned entirely with establishing identities, is unrecognized by Malcolm—who identified him smartly for Duncan in I.ii, and who here adds a little more gratuitous bulk and gratuitous delay to the scene by nattering about his brief difficulty in recognizing Ross. Ross is understandably unwilling to deliver the crushing news he brings Macduff. And, when Ross does at last approach the painful topic of Macduff's family, Macduff has to coax the information from him. Ross's well-intentioned reticence thus stretches out his own anguish and Macduff's and also heightens our sense of the horror of Macbeth's crime and of the pathos of Macduff's situation. Moreover, Ross's reticence also heightens the already aggravated lesser agony the scene inflicts on us as audience.

Ross delays doing what we assume or suspect he has come on stage to do, and Shakespeare provides conversational accidents that help Ross delay and make our frustration as audience comparable—on its lesser scale—to Macduff's. For example, when Macduff encourages Ross to speak further about his wife and children ("Be not a niggard of your speech. How goes't?"—180), Ross's answer seems on its way to telling Madcuff his family is dead: "When I came hither to transport the tidings / Which I have heavily borne, there ran a rumor / of . . . ." But the rumor is not the one we guess (and, as it at last turns out, rightly guess) Ross has heard—the rumor that Madcuff's castle has been surprised and his wife and babes savagely slaughtered. Ross will not get to that rumor for another twenty tortuous lines. The rumor he reports here is "Of many worthy fellows that were out" (183)—a rumor he pursues through a thicket of syntactically snarled modification ("Which was to my belief witnessed the rather / For that I saw the tyrant's power afoot"), to emerge at an exhortation to Malcolm to invade Scotland *promptly.* Ross's speech takes us back to a matter settled in the first half of the scene and leaves us further from the report we expect than we were ten lines earlier, when Macduff asked specifically about his wife and children.

Obviously, it is theatrically splendid that Shakespeare should so manipulate Ross's compassionately intended, but effectively torturous, reticence that it evokes an audience response parallel with the response it evokes from Macduff in the fiction. However, without denying the theatrical energy the delay generates, it is also true that the experience of these lines is unpleasant for an audience—unpleasant in very much the way any scene is when it drags.

What is more, Shakespeare develops the socially and emotionally awkward exchange between Ross and Macduff in such a way that it resembles the work of a clumsy playwright. Not only does Macduff have to prod Ross, he does so in lines that lack verisimilitude and seem prompted by the despair of a writer who does not know his trade. Ross has said that the words he has to speak are too painful to be heard; Macduff responds:

> What concern they,
> The general cause or is it a fee-grief
> Due to some single breast?
>
> [195—97]

Shakespeare's handling of Ross's delay also generates and prolongs a petty but real agony of understanding for us—for us who saw the slaughter but do not immediately know whether Ross knows what we know. Ross left the previous scene while Lady Macduff and her children were indeed "well at peace" (179)—were still alive and in good health. We do not know how to respond to Ross's answers when he tells Macduff that his family is "well" (177). Is this the traditional pious equivocation by which, because they are at rest and free of worldly cares, "we use / To say the dead are well" (*Antony and Cleopatra* II.v.32—33)—or is Ross merely reporting what he ignorantly believes to be simple fact—or is he insisting upon a quibbling distinction between the news he has heard and the now-superseded facts he knows at first hand? We are obliged to wait to find out.

To conclude this account of IV.iii, it should suffice to say that, when, immediately after IV.ii has closed on Lady Macduff's offstage cry of "Murder," we are presented with Macduff and Malcolm, we are thereby promised a scene that will show us Macduff's response to his private griefs and tell us what practical plans and hopes Malcolm and Macduff have for opposing Macbeth. The scene fulfills its promise, but in so frustrating a way that, from the beginning of the scene on-ward, an audience's experience includes impatience.[6] Malcolm and Macduff are and remain our allies, but in the morally insignifi-cant terms of our likes and dislikes as audience to an entertainment they are—because this scene is—irritating to us.[7]

In three scenes—V.ii, V.iv, and V.vi—between IV.iii and the death of Macbeth, Shakespeare gives us further opportunities to think of the action from the point of view of Malcolm, Macduff, and their army of liberation; he makes each of those opportunities uninviting. The scenes not only delay us in our variously certain progress toward the play's inevitable conclusion, they are, like IV.iii, slow in them-selves.

The first of the three, V.ii, serves an expository purpose: Menteith, Angus, Caithness, and Lennox inform us that Malcolm's invading army will soon reach Dunsinane and that Macbeth has fortified it against a siege. The scene also teases us with matter-of-fact references to Birnam Wood as the place where the Scottish patriots are to join forces with Malcolm. We know from all previous literary experience that the comfortable impossibilities the witches presented as the only threats to Macbeth will occur (just as the first people to hear the stories of Oedipus and of Rumplestiltskin presumably "knew" that Oedipus would murder his father and marry his mother and that the miller's daughter would somehow manage to spin gold from straw). Act V, scene ii both activates our eagerness to find out how Birnam Wood will manage to do the impossible and—because the scene me-anders for twenty extra lines—frustrates our desire. In the first speech of V.ii we hear that "revenges burn" in Malcolm, Siward, and MacDuff, but there is no fire in the placid chat of the thanes who tell us so; note, for instance, the ironically leisurely anaphoric use of *Now*'s in Angus's speculative account of Macbeth's state of mind:

> Now does he feel
> His secret murders sticking on his hands.
> Now minutely revolts upbraid his faith-breach.

Those he commands move only in command,
Nothing in love. Now does he feel his title
Hang loose about him, like a giant's robe
Upon a dwarfish thief.

[V.ii. 16–22]

Our next chance to defect from emotional commitment to Macbeth comes in V.iv, which follows the pattern of V.ii. The business of the scene is finished during its first seven lines:

Siward. What wood is this before us?
Menteith.   The Wood of Birnam.
Malcolm. Let every soldier hew him down a bough
    And bear't before him. Thereby shall we shadow
    The numbers of our host and make discovery
    Err in report of us.

[V.iv. 3–7]

The scene goes on for another fourteen lines, concluding with Siward's word-heavy commendation of finality:

                    The time approaches
That will with due decision make us know
What we shall say we have and what we owe.
Thoughts speculative their unsure hopes relate,
But certain issue strokes must arbitrate—
Towards which advance the war.
                    Exeunt, marching.

[V.iv. 16–21]

The last of the three scenes that offer us a chance to think of the battle from the viewpoint of the forces of virtue is V.vi, a scene ten lines long that does its scarcely necessary business in its first line ("Now near enough. Your leafy screens throw down") and then spends itself on prebattle formalities and rhyming rant. Such formalities and rant are usual before Shakespearean battles and are usually effective in generating excitement. Here the prophesied approach of Birnam Wood and the approach of one member of the army—Macduff—matter, but the army and its affairs are dramatically irrelevant to a climax for which the terms have been firmly established as supernatural. Shakespeare may have had extradramatic purpose in these scenes; for instance, a Jacobean audience probably found political edification in the play's insistence upon the family tie between the

English Siward and his Scottish nephew Malcolm; but, dramatically, Shakespeare's expense of attention on Siward must always have been an unwelcome diversion for audiences.[8]

The whole paradox I have been demonstrating—the paradox of audiences' dual contrary allegiances in *Macbeth*—is mirrored in a summary example provided in the issue of the speed at which the play moves. *Macbeth* moves so quickly and is therefore so short that scholars used to speculate carelessly on a lost "full" text of the play—a text of which the *Macbeth* we have was assumed to be only a mutilated relic. Such scholars may, of course, have been right, but the historically evident power the play has over audiences and the contribution speed makes to that power suggest that brevity was probably always the soul of the play.

Like Macbeth and the servant who outdistances him as they gallop ahead to bring Lady Macbeth news of Duncan's imminent arrival, the events of the play move at breakneck speed. I bring the matter up here because audiences like speed and because scenes with Macbeth in them never drag. As I have already suggested, the only exceptions to the rule of haste are the scenes that focus on Macbeth's virtuous victims and adversaries. In the theatre, speed is good and slowness is bad. In the story of Macbeth as staged by Shakespeare, virtuous characters and virtuous actions move slowly; speed is characteristic of the play's evil actions and their actors. What an audience approves in one dimension of its experience is at perfect odds with what it approves in another. One might say of an audience to *Macbeth* what Oswald says of Albany in *King Lear:* "What most he should dislike seems pleasant to him; / What like, offensive" (IV.ii.10−11).

Given what I have been saying for the last several pages, the following lines from *Macbeth* might well be describing the audience that hears them:

> But cruel are the times when we are traitors
> And do not know ourselves; when we hold rumor
> From what we fear, yet know not what we fear
> But float upon a wild and violent sea
> Each way and move.[9]

[IV.ii.18−22]

The trouble with such a neat summary critical conclusion is that, though it is just, it can, like my whole disquisition on the audience's tragically double orientation, seem to imply that audiences take conscious note of and are actively upset by the conflict between the locally active values they exercise from moment to moment as consumers of a dramatic product and the larger ones from which our culture traditionally evaluates human behavior. Obviously, nothing of the sort occurs. Audiences *like* attending *Macbeth;* we pay to go back and see it again when we can. For audiences, their times in the theatre with *Macbeth* are not cruel at all, and—unlike Albany—members of audiences to *Macbeth* show no signs of feeling the need to say "Great thing of us forgot" about their temporarily mislaid priorities. In fact, they do not mislay their moral priorities. Those priorities coexist comfortably with equally powerful, lesser, local, special ones during an effectively miraculous experience of practical paradox. That, indeed, is my point. I still claim validity for the hyperbolically stated proposition that the tragedy of plays like *Macbeth* occurs in the audience; but the tragic experience of audiences, though real, is not only bearable but as easily managed as flies are by the gods.

This is, thus, the proper point at which to reintroduce the distinction between our perceptions of artistically unmediated tragedy in ordinary experience and our experience of dramatic tragedy. Those plays that we agree belong in the category "tragedy"—those that strike us as having the particular but hard-to-particularize quality we call tragic and for which we are so grateful—are plays that admit into a comfortable mental experience responses that would ordinarily put us in a quandary—plays that admit such responses without disturbing our equanimity, or even our complacence, and admit them without denying or diminishing their virulence.

Like every work of art—from the humblest drawing or tune or sentence to Michelangelo's *David,* Beethoven's fourteenth quartet, or *Pride and Prejudice*—a dramatic tragedy is an enabling act. And, as we value works of art in proportion to the magnitude of the comprehensive power they confer upon us, so we traditionally give particularly high value to tragedy and the highest to successful tragedies. The glory of such a play as *Macbeth* is in its power as an enabling act—one by which we are not merely relieved of physical involvement in the dangerous events enacted before us (that minor felicity, after all, is ours whenever we see newsreels of disasters), but by which we are also genuinely, though temporarily, as we would be if we were superior to the sovereign fact of the human condition—superior to the helpless relativism in which the human mind is trapped and by virtue of which the human mind ordinarily requires itself to recognize one of the set of terms in which a perceived fact operates and to ignore or deny the others.

For the length of *Macbeth,* we are creatures so free of psychological dependence upon our fragile, dikelike belief in limits that our minds are not only comfortable but graceful in conditions that would ordinarily drive us mad to define our positions. For the length of *Macbeth* we are like superhuman beings, creatures capable of being mentally comfortable with infinite possibility. No wonder we enjoy ourselves.

I said earlier that an audience to *Macbeth* cannot keep itself within the category dictated by its own morality, even though its moral judgments are dictated entirely by that morality. The achievement of the play is that it enables its audience to endure the experience of such potential in itself.

By "experience of such potential," however, I do not mean—as I might seem to mean—"experience of *recognizing* such potential." I suggest, indeed, that the triumphant mental superiority I postulate for audiences to *Macbeth* is possible only *because* they are oblivious to the logical conflict in their responses and to their achievement in tolerating its irresolution.

If audiences were led to take conscious notice of the inconsistency in their evaluations of Macbeth or of Malcolm, they would presumably set about rationalizing their situations in an effort to make their responses consistent with one another by, for example, insisting that their thinking be governed by the indisputable precedence proper to the large, moral terms in which we must condemn Macbeth and cherish Malcolm—terms by comparison to which the transitory, local, merely theatrical terms in which Macbeth pleases and Malcolm displeases us are too petty to bother about.

Since the clash between two powerful, urgent, differently based sets of judgments remains only potential, an audience's experience of *Macbeth* contains—has wrapped within its fabric—a token experience of being able to cope with conflicts comparable to those our minds cannot cope with, those that cannot be placed and managed in a single frame of reference. In *Macbeth,* as in the few other great tragedies that give us the special joy *Macbeth* gives us, our token experience of superiority to dependence on the mental machinations by which we customarily define and redefine the thus diminished elements of experience and make it manageable is particularly persuasive because it occurs in company with contemplation of a dramatized story full of events and situations that are in fact beyond the mental control of the characters they involve. The experience of *Macbeth* testifies to its audience's mental capacity to survive mental challenges as demanding as the ones that overwhelm Macbeth—and overwhelm Lady Macbeth and, on a lesser scale, Macduff, Lady Macduff, and their mentally self-confident, mentally foolhardy little boy.

Perhaps the grounds for the high value I put on unobserved conflict will be clear if I introduce two lesser conflicts involved in (wrapped up within) *Macbeth,* conflicts comparable to our conflicting judgments on Macbeth and on Malcolm only in going unobserved.

The play enables its audiences wholly to miss the glaring but invisible ludicrousness of the double standard by which Macbeth evaluates supernatural predictions. He takes those favorable to his hopes as revelations of unalterable fate; thus he announces his confidence that he is immune to danger from all persons born of woman and that he is safe until Birnam Wood comes to Dunsinane. On the other hand, he assumes that he has it within his power to prevent the seed of Banquo from growing to be kings. Our minds also live comfortably with unexploited irony in the fact that Macbeth, who has reason to fear Macduff and Banquo's children, succeeds in murdering Banquo and Macduff's children.

Although anyone's schoolroom experiences will suggest that the stuff of ironies has effect only as it is observed to be so, I submit that the raw materials for these two unobserved ironies do more for us by being unobserved than they would if the playwright had pointed them up and insisted that we notice them.[10]

An irony differs radically from the raw materials that compose it and are composed within it. In formulating an irony we bring its elements under control, remove most of their energy—exactly the disconcerting energy that impels us to master conflicting facts in a neat paradoxical assertion by which they take on a fixed, composite single identity, albeit identity as an anomaly. Irony derives from collision, and a collision gives psychologically palpable unity to the colliding forces, which we can comprehend in relation to the point at which they collide.

Because *Macbeth* evokes conflicting responses that could but do not collide in our consciousnesses, and because it both includes and omits to exploit logical inconsistencies in its characters' behavior, the experience of seeing or reading *Macbeth* is experience of an object that is under constant pressure from within—an object full of volatile elements always ready to meet and explode.

Macbeth makes us able to sit unperturbed in the presence of mutually antipathetic facts of a sort that in ordinary experience put our minds in panic when we so much as suspect that they coexist. The play can give us our unwonted tolerance for unresolved energy because, although limitless in effectively numberless dimensions, *Macbeth* is limited in at least as many more.

The limits—the means by which the play assures us that, however open-ended it may be, it is *also* a three-hour object whose elements so pertain to one another that it has thinglike identity, a beginning, a middle, and an end that are not arbitrary—are achieved in patterns of substantive incidentals so insistent and so profuse that our minds are emboldened to accept irresolution in the large matters that concern us and to which we devote our attention.

The events depicted in *Macbeth* are not complete, not a closed unit with a beginning, a middle, and an end. Similarly, an audience's experience of *Macbeth* is of truth beyond the limits of categories. That experience, which I think is what we are labeling when we use the word *tragedy,* is made bearable by a vehicle, the fabric of the play, which has limits, has pattern, and is insistently man-made. The patterns of the play are made by the very elements whose disjunction takes the mind beyond the usual limits of its tolerance. Some of them I have already touched on; others have been the stuff of modern criticism for the last fifty years: things like image patterns in clothes, drink, babies, and blood; echoes of one situation in another; resemblances of characters to one another; recurrent themes; and so on.

I will, however, mention one such pattern. A good emblem for the failure of categories in *Macbeth* would be "Fair is foul, and foul is fair" at the end of scene i. An echo of that statement occurs as Macbeth's first line at the beginning of scene iii: "So foul and fair a day I have not seen." The paired consonantal sounds in "fair" and "foul" make a surprisingly sustained, complex alliterative pattern that runs across the whole play—a nonsignifying pattern in "far," "fear," "free," "file," "fail," "fall," "fool," "false" . . . a quietly sustaining pattern that is only literally *full* of sound and *fury* and that, though it signifies nothing, helps a sane human mind experience tragedy—live with essentially unmediated truth—and survive. What *Macbeth* does for us—what successful dramatic tragedy does for us—is like what the word *tragedy* does for real-life tragedies: it gives local habitation and a name to the most terrifying of things, "a deed without a name" (IV.i.49), without denying its namelessness, its incomprehensibility, its indefinition.

APPENDIX 1:
ON THE PERSISTENCE
OF FIRST IMPRESSIONS

My discussions of the plays I have talked about have made no allowance whatever for distinctions between first impressions of a play and the responses of audiences who already know the play well. For instance, most modern audiences have read *King Lear* before they see it—or at least know enough about it and its reputation to know that this play that does in fact forget about one of its major characters (the Fool, after his exit from III.vi) will not forget about Lear and Cordelia and will not—as it threatens to do—conclude while their careers are still unresolved. And yet, I speak as if I saw no significant difference between the moment-to-moment responses of audiences to whom *King Lear* is an unknown quantity and those of audiences who have seen the play before or read it or heard about its troublesome ending. I do in fact see little difference between the two.

To say that is to speak against the advice of common sense, which insists that, once one knows how something "comes out," one's responses to it will be determined in passage by one's knowledge of what is to come in a sentence, a scene, or a story.

But consider riddles. No literary object seems more likely to lose its initial effect than a riddle is after it is answered. Consider this riddle: "What is black and white and red all over?" Every English-speaking person over ten years of age presumably knows the answer—a newspaper—and has known it for some time. Moreover, most English-speakers who were schoolchildren in the nineteen-forties and fifties also know the differently witty alternative answer: *The Daily Worker,* an answer that duplicates the standard answer (*The Daily Worker* was a newspaper—was read), and runs the original wordplay backwards, depending on abandonment of the original pun (on "red" and "read") for the extra energy acquired by its own pun (on the color red in its literal sense and in its political one).

I submit that, no matter how familiar one is with the simple paradox (what is black and white can also be red, but cannot be entirely red) and its pun-based solution, one's mind still follows the familiar path through bewilderment—even if one retraces it at so high a speed that one instantly snaps the answer back at the cruelly

disappointed preschool child who posed the riddle. The same is true,
I think, for the comparatively baroque steps from the simple riddle,
through its traditional answer, to *The Daily Worker*.

In *King Lear* something similar happens—at least to me—when,
after Goneril and Albany have met Regan and Edmund to join the
two English armies in opposition against the French invader, Goneril
concludes the following exchange by saying "I know the riddle":

> *Regan.* Sister, you'll go with us?
> *Goneril.* No.
> *Regan.* 'Tis most convenient. Pray go with us.
> *Goneril.* O ho, I know the riddle. — I will go.
>
> [V.i.34—37]

I long ago saw that Goneril's exit line means "I understand why
Regan makes an issue of my leaving here when she does: she does not
want me to have a chance to be alone with Edmund." Nonetheless,
every time Goneril says, "I know the riddle," my mind says, "*I do
not.*" That response occurs, and I expect it always will, even though it
is instantly superseded by the answer I reached long ago when I first
wondered what Goneril meant.

Similarly, though perhaps idiosyncratically, I am always surprised
and usually momentarily hopeful when Desdemona, who has seemed
dead for several minutes, suddenly revives at V.ii.118 of *Othello*.
(Once, years ago and by accidents of scheduling and geography, I saw
a different production of *Othello* every night for five nights. During
the last scene of the fourth of the five productions I noticed the
curious persistence of my surprise and hope when Desdemonas come
back momentarily to life. My self-consciousness carried over to the
next night, and I experienced neither surprise when that evening's
Desdemona cried out to Emilia nor my usual flicker of logically
inexplicable hope that, just this once, Desdemona will survive. However, when I saw *Othello* again several months later, my self-conscious
bemusement had faded: I got caught up in the play and, as usual, was
surprised and encouraged by Desdemona's revival—even though
those responses immediately evoked self-mocking recollections of my
previous observations on the phenomenon.)

Narratively crucial surprises, however, are a different matter. They
work only once. By narratively crucial surprises I mean surprises like
the one that occurs in Alfred Hitchcock's *The 39 Steps* when the

avuncular ally in whose house the fugitive hero has apparently found safety reveals himself to be the master criminal whose only known distinguishing characteristic is a mutilated finger, and like the surprise that occurs in Agatha Christie's *And Then There Were None* when a reader finds out how ten murders can have been committed, although the ten victims are the only possible suspects. The pleasure to be had from such surprises is great, but is not necessarily preeminent. Sometimes it is: *And Then There Were None* is my favorite mystery story, but I have no inclination to reread it. More often the pleasure of the surprise is not preeminent: I like to see *The 39 Steps* every year or so. Similarly, many people regularly reread or resee *Bleak House, Pride and Prejudice, War and Peace,* and *Othello*—even though they already know how Tulkinghorn died, know that Lydia will elope with Wickham, know who Natasha finally marries, and know that weaponless Othello will stab himself to death in the course of an unexpectedly leisurely anecdote about a bygone incident at Aleppo.

The argument that one can still enjoy a narrative after one knows its crucial secrets is too familiar and too just to need rehearsal here. I bring it up only as an auxiliary to a related but different argument, the argument that *non*crucial literary mysteries and surprises recur indefinitely in audiences already well acquainted with the works in which they occur—the argument that every time one reads or sees the works I listed one reexperiences one's ignorance—and reexercises one's suspicions about Tulkinghorn's murderer, is shocked at Lydia's newly unexpected elopement, is delighted that Natasha should once again have had the wisdom to accept Pierre, and is as moved as ever at the eternally unexpected action Othello takes when he says, "I took by th' throat the circumcised dog / And smote him—thus."

Some support for the proposition that one's first experience of a literary object recurs in those that follow is apparent in the commonly observable fact that one can fear for the welfare of characters threatened by disasters—for instance, heroines strapped to railroad tracks or heroes dangling from ledges—even when one has seen the movie before and knows that they escape unharmed. Those two stock hypothesized instances are, of course, not ideal, because, even on one's first time through, one's real fears coexisted with generic assurance that heroes and heroines always survive such trials.

A better example would be a rereader's experience of such a generically complex literary situation as the one in which Isabell Archer decides not to marry Lord Warburton. I submit that any reader who on first reading the first pages of *Portrait of a Lady* hoped Isabel would marry Warburton feels that hope during each successive reading— even though that same reader consciously remembers the transformation and elevation of a reader's ambition for Isabel that is worked during the long account of her character and her values that intervenes between the novel's first scene and the rejection of Warburton's offer of marriage. In that first brief scene, three gentlemen—one of whom is wealthy, charming, titled, and maritally eligible—await the impending arrival of Isabel, a young American girl, a heroine apparently suited to the mold from which have come Cinderella, Elizabeth Bennet, Jane Eyre, the heroine of *Rebecca,* and Our Gal Sunday (heroine of an American radio serial of the nineteen-thirties and forties; her story "asked the question, can this girl from a simple mining town in the West find happiness as the wife of Britain's richest and most handsome lord?"). Granting that any reader who has once read much past the first chapter of *Portrait of a Lady* knows that Isabel cannot be held within the dowdy terms of pulp fiction, I still suspect that at Isabel's first appearance at the end of chapter 1 rereaders once again recognize her as generically destined to power a novel that presents her predictably awkward and predictably successful journey to domestic tranquility as Lady Warburton—a novel Henry James does not write but which is, and in each rereading continues to be, the route by which we are led into the novel James does give us.

I submit that a similar recapitulation of original responses occurs when a previously initiated audience meets Edmund, the once and future villain of *King Lear,* in scene i, where he is and will always seem the meek victim of his father's brutal jocularity—and when, at the beginning of scene ii, Edmund unexpectedly reveals himself to be the Machiavel the audience remembers him to be. And, I think, audiences who know that Marcade will enter suddenly in the last moments of *Love's Labor's Lost* and turn its course awry always retrace the familiar mental path from surprise at Marcade's entrance to reorientation in the new situation his news brings into being. I would say much the same about Prospero's perennially unexpected disruption of the masque he presents for Ferdinand and Miranda (*Tempest* IV.i.139–42), and—on a smaller scale—about Hamlet's comically perverse replies to Polonius (replies like "Words, words, words" in response to "What do you read, my lord?" [II.ii.190–91], and " 'By and by' is easily said" in response to "I will say so," Polonius's answer when Hamlet said "I will come by and by" [III.ii.369−72]).

How it is that we are capable of such reexperience does not much matter. The reason we can do it, I think, is that, as a familiar literary construct passes across our understandings, the promissory signals that deceived us the first time still signal what they signaled the first time and evoke again the expectations they evoked before, evoke them in us even when those expectations coexist with knowledge that they will be frustrated. Thus *King Lear* will continue forever and for all of us to move toward a happy ending in which Lear and Cordelia live happily ever after. Thus, also, Rosaline's couplet beginning "Since you are strangers and come here by chance, / We'll not be nice: take hands . . ." (*Love's Labor's Lost* V.ii. 219−20), will always promise to conclude with "and we will dance"—even for an audience that has known since its sophomore survey course in Shakespeare that Rosaline's couplet unexpectedly ends with "we will not dance," an audience that, though surprised by the familiar perversity of the response, would, in another dimension of understanding, be even more surprised to hear an actress actually give the simultaneously expected and unexpected positive answer toward which Rosaline's sentence points.

What matters much more than why we are capable of such compli-cated reexperience is establishing the fact that we *do* regularly un-dergo such reexperiences. And that fact, unfortunately, is one that cannot be established. I will, I imagine, always have to contend unsuccessfully with students and reviewers who, very logically, insist that all one's experiences of a work that succeed the first are radically different from the first, *are* different only because they logically *must* be—who insist that, once one knows the destination a phrase, a sentence, a speech, a poem, a novel, or a play actually reaches, one's mind no longer follows signals that beckon elsewhere. I earlier referred to this essay as an argument. It is not, however, really an argument but a plea—an appeal away from common sense to what I strongly suspect is common knowledge, logically inconvenient common knowledge derived from logically improbable common experience.

APPENDIX 2:
SPECULATIONS ON DOUBLING
IN SHAKESPEARE'S PLAYS

Your If is the only peace-maker; much virtue in If.

Cordelia and Lear's Fool never meet on stage, and ever since Wilfred Perrett's *The Story of King Lear* in 1904 critics have often and persuasively argued that one boy actor played both parts. *If* that was indeed the case, then "And my poor fool is hanged," the statement with which Lear begins his last speech, takes on an extra dimension in a scene and play notable for irreverence of definitions and ideational boundaries. Inasmuch as the possibility of such a dimension to *King Lear* has so long been a relatively tame familiar among Shakespearians, I hope that it may evoke some tolerance for the following pure but not wholly wanton speculation on phenomena of which "And my poor fool" may be the ultimate instance: Shakespeare's awareness and use of the dramatic potential in the fact of performance and the facts of particular performances.

The facts of playhouse, actors, costumes—all the accidents of performance—can never be absent from the mind of an audience, but in our willingness to suspend disbelief we ordinarily maintain a separating membrane between our consciousness of the events portrayed and our consciousness of the actual theatrical events that convey the story. The partition is easily breached—by fat heroines, fire engines in the street outside, forgotten lines, inadequate props, an over- or underheated theatre, or the accidental pertinence of a word, line, or situation to some concern local to a particular time, place, or audience (I once saw a Petruchio who came back after intermission without his glass eye); but our minds ordinarily reject incursions of playhouse reality into the fiction. We simply amend performances in passage in much the way we automatically correct or delete linotypers' errors while we read a newspaper. We entertain two fused but distinct "realities" at once.

Shakespeare seems always to have been fascinated with the double consciousness inherent in watching actors on a stage and watching the characters they portray. His interest is most straightforwardly evident in the opening chorus of *Henry V*. More typically, however, Shake-

speare likes to experiment with the unsettling but enriching effects to
be had from making an audience's two incompatible consciousnesses
indivisible. Take, for example, his inexhaustible delight in the fact of
boys playing girls who are pretending to be boys (in *As You Like It* he
treats us to the contemplation of a boy pretending to be a girl pretending to be a boy pretending to be a girl,[1] or such exercises as a
scene where two actors playing antique Danes discuss a "late inno-
vation" of a London theatre *in* a London theatre during a "war of
the theatres" in which both speakers are combatants (*Hamlet*
II.ii.320−54), or a scene where an actor playing a Danish prince
gives an acting lesson to a group of actors playing actors (*Hamlet*
III.ii.1−42). In the scene where Julius Caesar is murdered, the actor
playing Cassius speculates on a future that is also the present: "How
many ages hence / Shall this our lofty scene be acted over / In states
unborn and accents yet unknown" (*Julius Caesar* III.i. 111−13). At
the very end of *Antony and Cleopatra* the boy playing Cleopatra delivered this excellent description of the first scenes of the performance in
which he spoke it:

> The quick comedians
> Extemporally will stage us, and present
> Our Alexandrian revels: Antony
> Shall be brought drunken forth, and I shall see
> Some squeaking Cleopatra boy my greatness
> I' th' posture of a whore.
>
> [V.ii. 216−21]

In a scene where actors pretending to be Toby Belch, Maria, and
Fabian mock the pretentious Malvolio by pretending they believe he
is mad, Fabian says, "If this were played upon a stage now, I could
condemn it as an improbable fiction" (*Twelfth Night* III.iv. 119−20).
Even in *Henry V*, where the chorus begins by carefully distinguishing
between what the audience sees on the stage and what is represented
there, he goes on to mock the distinction with a pun on real and
metaphoric nausea:

> . . . the scene
> Is now transported, gentles, to Southampton.
> There is the playhouse now, there must you sit,
> And thence to France shall we convey you safe
> And bring you back, charming the narrow seas

To give you gentle pass; for, if we may,
We'll not offend one stomach with our play.

[II.Chorus.34—40]

The general phenomenon probably reaches its ultimate complexity in
Thisby's logically casual, joyously obscene, "I kiss the wall's hole, not
your lips at all" (*A Midsummer Night's Dream* V.i.199).

Shakespeare's demonstrable experimentation with unifications of
performance and performed invites speculation on other and non-
demonstrable experiments along the same lines—notably by means of
doubling parts. We know of instances where Renaissance companies
did double parts,[2] and we know (from such things as the tracks of a
tall blond boy actor and a short dark one in the early comedies), that
Shakespeare wrote with his casts in mind. We are also mindful of
characters like Francisco, Philo, and Archidamus, who appear in the
first scenes of their plays and vanish;[3] of characters like Poins and
Casca, who are important in the early parts of plays and absent
thereafter; and of important characters like the Earl of Douglas, Octavius (in *Julius Caesar*), and Macduff, who do not speak until others
have strutted their hours and departed. Speculation on doubled parts
has traditionally served to explain such mysterious appearances and
disappearances; it could also explain why *As You Like It* has two dukes
named Frederick and two characters named Oliver (see Oliver
Mar-Text's uncalled-for exit lines in III.iii). Speculation on doubling
might also lead to more far-reaching possible connections between
Shakespeare's activities as writer and his activities as producer.

Consider the explosion of categories effected by the following exchange if the actors playing Titania and Oberon double as Hippolyta
and Theseus:

Oberon. Ill met by moonlight, proud Titania.
Titania. What, jealous Oberon? Fairy, skip hence.
   I have forsworn his bed and company.
Oberon. Tarry, rash wanton. Am not I thy lord?
Titania. Then I must be thy lady; but I know
   When thou hast stolen away from fairyland,
   And in the shape of Corin sat all day,
   Playing on pipes of corn, and versing love
   To amorous Phillida. Why art thou here,
   Come from the farthest steep of India,
   But that, forsooth, the bouncing Amazon,

Your buskined mistress and your warrior love,
To Theseus must be wedded, and you come
To give their bed joy and prosperity?
Oberon. How canst thou thus, for shame, Titania,
Glance at my credit with Hippolyta,
Knowing I know thy love to Theseus?
Didst thou not lead him through the glimmering night
From Perigenia, whom he ravished?
And make him with fair Aegles break his faith,
With Ariadne, and Antiopa?
Titania. These are the forgeries of jealousy . .
. . . .
And through this distemperature we see
The seasons alter: hoary-headed frosts
Fall in the fresh lap of the crimson rose,
And on old Hiems' thin and icy crown
An odorous chaplet of sweet summer buds
Is, as in mockery, set. The spring, the summer,
The childing autumn, angry winter change
Their wonted liveries; and the mazed world,
By their increase, now knows not which is which . . .
[*MND* II.i.60−81, 106−14]

I begin with the example of the royal couples in *A Midsummer
Night's Dream* for several reasons: (1) because the possibility that one
pair of actors played both couples is specifically—though, I believe,
arbitrarily—denied by William Ringler in the most sophisticated,
recent, respectable, and respected of all studies of Shakespearian
doubling;[4] (2) because doubling in those four roles (and in those of
Philostrate and Puck) in Peter Brook's 1971 Royal Shakespeare Company production was so spectacularly workable and so spectacularly
successful as to have since become a theatrical fad among less grand
companies; (3) because in Brook's production the entrance of Theseus
and Hippolyta at IV.i.102, immediately after the same actors have
exited as Oberon and Titania at IV.i.101—the entrance that caused
Ringler to say that the kings and queens could not have been successfully doubled—particularly delighted the two audiences I observed as
they watched the Brook production and also seemed to delight the
two actors (who strode back through the doorway grinning in apparent triumph at the transparent theatricality of their physically minimal metamorphosis); and—most importantly—(4) because the lines

quoted above suggest that they were written to capitalize on and intensify the effect of planned theatrical doubling.

The lines (which lead up to the dispute over the changeling boy), seem specially designed to hold a maximum number and variety of examples of changes and confusions of persona: Oberon and Titania dwell on identity (". . . Am not I thy lord?" "Then I must be thy lady . . ."). Titania alludes to a magical metamorphosis in Oberon's shape and to the season's improbable changes of costume. She introduces the topic of Oberon's infidelity with Phillida, and that accusation merges muddily with the charge of infidelity with Hippolyta. Oberon accuses Titania of alienating Theseus's affections from three lovers whom he had abandoned in the past; the abandonment of "Aegles" and Ariadne is clearly documented in mythology, but in some accounts "Antiopa" is another name for Hippolyta herself (Plutarch calls her Antiope, and, in the course of recording the various and conflicting accounts of Theseus's campaigns against the Amazons, says this—here in North's version: "Clidemus the Historiographer . . . sayeth that . . . peace was taken betwene them by meanes of one of the women called Hyppolita. For this Historiographer calleth the Amazone which Theseus maried, Hyppolita, and not Antiopa").

Despite the scholarly enlightenment we have undergone during the last hundred years, most of our thinking about Elizabethan casting is still based on the assumed universality of modern practices. Moreover, we show a narrowmindedness improbable in a century that accepted Charlie Chaplin as monochromatic, mute, twenty feet high, and flat. We are inclined, for example, to assume that young actors played young characters and that changes of costume and make-up were radical and time-consuming. What if characters "were to be known by garment, not by favor?" By analogy with the George Spelvins and Walter Plinges who used to skulk through the cast lists of twentieth-century barnstormers, we generally assume that Elizabethan companies doubled parts as a last resort when they were understaffed. We take it for granted that a Lawrence Olivier or a John Wayne will always play the best parts in any productions in which he appears; we are untroubled that the General Burgoyne of this week's play was Othello last week and Archie Rice before that. What if Elizabethan audiences exercised the same habits of mind not only between play and play but between scene and scene, so that a leading actor's assignments within a single play were limited by nothing but physical possibility and the egos of his peers? What if Bottom's ridiculous scheme for playing Pyramus and Thisbe and the lion were slightly less of an exaggeration of Elizabethan stage practice than it now seems?

I suspect that Shakespeare used the doubling of parts in performance adjectivally—to inform, comment on, and, perhaps, augment the events enacted. For example, although I do not accept the casual premises on which Ringler rejects the possibility of doubling the royal couples in *A Midsummer Night's Dream,* I am at least as much persuaded as Ringler himself is by his well-documented and carefully argued suggestion (pp. 133−34) that the four adult actors who played Flute, Snout, Starveling, and Snug doubled as Peaseblossom, Cobweb, Moth, and Mustardseed. The doubling of those contrasting sets of roles in production mirrors, underscores, and comments on the comically troublesome philosophic implications of the "doubling" of Flute, Snout, Starveling, and Snug—four "real" people—with Thisby, Wall, Moonshine, and Lion—the complexly and variously unreal creatures they personify in the play staged within the fiction.

Before I go further, I should acknowledge the fact that this essay has obviously invaded the traditional purviews of old-fashioned, hardcore literary scholarship; and—even though I have been, and will be, at pains to insist that my speculations are *only* speculations, that I do not pretend to be proving anything—I will pause to examine the validity of arguments inconvenient to my own which have been offered by earlier and more obviously qualified speculators—speculators who have believed themselves to have proved, or who have been believed to have proved, their cases. In picking at the work of my predecessors, I may seem to think I am discrediting it. I do not think that at all. I mean only to suggest that their arguments are as speculative as my own and are equally, and just as necessarily, selective and arbitrary both in their use of the sparse, inconsistent, and therefore inconclusive surviving evidence about Renaissance doubling practices and in their use of analogies from modern theatrical custom.

Inasmuch as I began with the case for doubling Cordelia and Lear's Fool, and since I will conclude there also, arguments against that possibility make a good point of departure for a survey of previous speculation. This is the immediately relevant portion of Kenneth Muir's note on "And my poor fool is hang'd" in the Arden *King Lear:* "Brandl, Quiller-Couch and Edith Sitwell have argued that the two parts of Cordelia and the Fool were taken by the same actor; but [Alwin] Thaler, *T.L.S.* 13 Feb. 1930 [p. 122], shows that the parts could not have been doubled."[5]

In fact, Thaler shows only that he believes such a doubling would not have been to his taste. I say "believes" because the immediate occasion of Thaler's letter to the *Times* was an Old Vic production of *Julius Caesar* in which "forty-three speaking parts (not counting the mob) were done by twenty-five players"; Thaler, who "did not happen to get a programme until the play was over" was delighted because he failed to detect a dozen instances of doubling. However, although he assumes that audiences are inevitably displeased when they recognize one actor in two or more roles, Thaler seems to have been equally delighted by the experience of detecting the reappearances of one actor who played Decius Brutus, Lepidus, and Messala. "The good round *voice*" of that "gifted and versatile actor . . . gave him away; but the trouble (if trouble it was) lay also in the fact that he was called upon to double—or rather, to treble—in parts which repeatedly gave him almost the centre of the stage, though not nearly so much prominence, after all, as the storm and agonies of Lear give to the Fool and to Cordelia."

The bases of Thaler's specific case against the doubling of the Fool and Cordelia are inferentially presented at the end of the foregoing excerpt; they are (1) that an audience would inevitably have been aware that the same actor played both parts, and (2) that doubling those parts or any others like them would therefore be aesthetically unsatisfying. I grant the first but not the second (with which Thaler himself seems uncomfortable; see his parenthetical "if trouble it was").

Thaler works also from a complementary set of casual and dubious assumptions about the desires and perquisites of actors, a set of assumptions which, like those about the likes and dislikes of audiences, had recently sustained the more prolix and more arbitrary speculations of William J. Lawrence in *Pre-Restoration Stage Studies* (Cambridge, Mass., 1927), pp. 43–78. Both Thaler and Lawrence assume that, in Thaler's words, "doubling was, at best, a necessary evil." As they work through the perfectly inconclusive available evidence, that assumption is embodied in a succession of "have to" constructions (e.g., this from Thaler: "Dr. Greg's analysis has shown . . . that not a few sharers in Henslowe's companies did have to double . . . as, for instance, in certain performances of Peele's *Battle of Alcazar* in which 26 actors did 60 parts, and the 'burden of doubling fell mainly on the sharers.' This, of course, does not absolutely prove that the sharers in Shakespeare's company also had to double, though it may not be altogether beside the point to observe that the principals in modern productions of Shakespeare . . . do not escape entirely").

The foregoing example focuses on a distinction between sharers and hired players that is urgent to the arguments of Thaler and Lawrence, a distinction that is, I think, misconceived because it rests on the improbable assumption that actors do not like performing. In obedience to a variation on the kind of snobbish, temporary prejudice that had earlier led less sophisticated commentators to such grosser follies as the conclusion that a mere actor from Stratford could not have written the plays that bear his name and the conclusion that, if he did write them, he must have been an inept and unwilling actor who appeared as infrequently as possible and then only in small, genteel roles—Thaler and Lawrence assume that Renaissance actors did not like doubling parts, that the extra work of doubling would have been onerous to them, and that doubling would have demeaned the doubler.

This is Lawrence explaining why he thinks "that the perfectly obvious 'doubles' in *Hamlet* were precisely those which were carefully avoided": "Though the necessary intermediate annihilation of a character might suggest to the dramatist how the services of the released actor might be further utilized, he would, I think, occasionally be given pause by the status of the actor. Polonius [whom 'modern barnstormers' often double with the First Gravedigger] and the Ghost [also a prime candidate for doubling] were important roles and must have been sustained by two sharers . . . Personally, I cannot see sharers trenching on the pitiful prerogative of the hirelings" (pp. 71–72). Personally, I can.

Lawrence's adverbial admission and my own are unavoidable and must be of the essence of any study of this subject. The evidence is insufficient to allow for anything like objectivity.

Even the hard evidence on Renaissance doubling practices is soft. Take, for example, the table of character distribution printed in the 1611 quarto of *The Fair Maid of the Exchange*. It purports to distribute twenty-one characters among eleven actors; its evidence suggests that doubling was not restricted to minor roles (the part of Barnard and three lesser parts are all listed "for one"); that actors doubled in very different roles (Barnard, an adult male, is listed for the same actor who plays two women and a boy); and that very fast changes were not considered impractical (the list demands that the actor who exits at line 601 as Bobbington, a thrasonical footpad, reenter three lines later as Mr. Berry, an elderly gentleman).

However, although the list testifies that prospective buyers of the 1611 quarto would have been unsurprised by such doubles, it calls for a demonstrably impossible production; as Lawrence points out (p. 75), both Barnard and Mr. Berry are onstage late in the play at the same time as characters whom the list says they double. The casting table is thus useful but treacherous evidence both for and against the belief that parts were freely doubled on the late sixteenth-century and early seventeenth-century London stage.[6] No conclusion can be other than speculative, and a speculator's direction necessarily reflects the brand of common sense that suits his personal aesthetic bias.

Thus, Lawrence—faced with one of the rare surviving cast lists, the Dramatis Personae published with the 1629 text of Massinger's *The Roman Actor*—treats the fact that a sharer in the King's company is listed for two roles as a mysterious deviation from custom: "fourteen players are shown taking sixteen characters [several characters are not listed], but curiously enough, though several hirelings played parts, the only doubling revealed fell to the lot of a sharer, T. Pollard, whose name stands opposite [those of two characters, Aelius Lamia and Stephanos]" (pp. 76–77). I, on the other hand, resist with difficulty an inclination to press Thomas Pollard's double duty into service as evidence for a hypothetical norm exactly opposite to Lawrence's. This particular speck of rare evidence especially appeals to me because it suggests that parts were doubled from choice as well as from necessity. Lawrence continues:

> This remarkable reversal of [what he assumes must have been] custom somewhat mystifies, but we have still another puzzle. Of the sixteen [listed] characters, four were sustained by boy players of women, though the adult players, sharers and hirelings, of the King's company certainly numbered more than twelve. Since the full manpower had not been drawn upon, what then the necessity for resort to doubling? It was not as if anything was gained by economizing in players: a sharer got his share even on days he did not act. [p. 77]

A similar divergence of interpretation results from contrary aesthetic perspectives on the induction to Marston's *Antonio and Mellida,* where some boy actors discuss the parts they are about to play. When asked what part he is to act, one of them replies, "The necessity of the play forceth me to act two parts: Andrugio, the distressed Duke of Genoa, and Alberto, a Venetian gentleman, enamoured on the Lady Rossaline" (ed. G. K. Hunter in the Regents Renaissance Drama Series [Lincoln, Nebraska, 1965], lines 21–23). Lawrence takes the speech as an "oblique apology," and, since doubling "cannot have been so rarely resorted to . . . as to necessitate any explanation or apology," he sees no reason for Marston to write the speech, "unless perchance it were that some exigency had compelled him to run counter to a recognized taboo and make the actor of so important a character as Andrugio double it with another" (p. 63).

I, on the other hand, see the induction as a sustained exposition —and exploitation—of the likenesses and unlikenesses of the various kinds of doubleness inherent in all acting, and particularly in acting a play in which actors pretend to be characters who pretend to be what they are not.

The boys discuss their parts: one is to play a hypocrite; another will play Antonio, a young nobleman who disguises himself as an amazon (in order to woo a boy actor playing a heroine who disguises herself as a page); another, when asked what part he plays, says, "The part of all the world," and then explains away that improbability by saying that by "the part of all the world" he means "the fool"; a fourth plays "a modern braggadoch"; and a fifth plays Galeatzo, "a right part for Proteus": "now . . . as grave as a Puritan's ruff; with the same breath as slight and scattered in his fashion as—as—as— a—a—anything . . . now lamenting, then chafing, straight laughing, then . . .".

In that group, the actor who says he plays two parts merely adds one more to a carefully baroque collection of doubles; and the inclusion of theatrical doubling in such a context suggests that at least one playwright saw (and, if only for the length of the induction to *Antonio and Mellida,* expected an audience to see) thematic ramifications in accidents of production—saw that theatrical doubling is akin to, has the same physics as, and is an exploitable auxiliary of the double identities that are the mainsprings of delight in all theatrical productions and most theatrical plots, delight in imperfectly blurred distinctions between such categories as fact/fiction, stage/fictional location, actor/character, child/adult, male/female, reality/disguise, honesty/hypocrisy, truth/falsehood, and wicked lies/innocent deception.

My sense of theatrical aesthetics says that Thaler and Lawrence base their commonsense arguments on assumptions that misunderstand the tastes of audiences and the temperament of actors. *My* common sense says that audiences have not changed much in four hundred years. The famous elegy on Burbage ascribed to "Jo ffletcher" suggests that, like us, Renaissance audiences delighted alternately and equally in being taken in by theatrical illusion and by seeing through it (and thus becoming party to it); the elegist revels both in listing contrasting characters in whom he has recognized Burbage ("young Hamlet, ould Heironymoe") and in the fact "that spectators . . . whilst he but seem'd to bleed, / Amazed, thought even then hee dyed in deed." Similarly, actors seem always to have delighted in the virtuosity involved in doubling—as Bottom and Holofernes, Shakespeare's fictional amateur actors, testify; as Hamlet suggests, professionals, too, probably wanted to do more and not less than was required of them—wished to speak more than was set down for them.

If I were to choose modern analogues, I would point (1) to Lon Chaney playing bit parts in films—and sometimes in scenes—where he played the star part; (2) to *Frankenstein Meets the Wolf Man* (Universal Pictures, 1943), in which Bela Lugosi was billed as, and in close-ups actually played, Frankenstein's Monster; Lugosi was by then too weak to carry the costume, so Lon Chaney, Jr. played both monsters through most of the film; (3) to the fact that people who detect that instance of doubling are delighted to do so and that, when they tell their friends, the friends are equally delighted by having been fooled; (4) to the London stage in 1957; in that year Robert Morley appeared in a play he seems to have reworked for the specific purpose of playing a portly middle-aged man and his portly young nephew (who at one point met each other in a doorway: one departed—balding and in a three-piece gray business suit—just as the other entered with bright red hair and wearing a sporty checkered jacket); in the same year Richard Attenborough appeared in a play that hinged on whether the central character did or did not have a criminal twin brother (once Attenborough exited, rear stage right, and—in what seemed less time than it would have taken him to run diagonally across the stage—sauntered from the wings at the front of the stage on the other side, totally recostumed as "the brother"); (5) to the fact that those two ridiculous plays offered nothing to Morley, Attenborough, or their audiences except delight in impossibly quick changes; and (6) to the fact that was quite enough to satisfy all parties.

If it is now thoroughly understood how genuinely speculative the enterprise must necessarily be, I will proceed to offer some possibilities for Shakespearian doubles that would thematically enrich the plays in which I propose them and that *might* have been not only anticipated but exploited as Shakespeare wrote. Each, like the doubles employed by Brook and those proposed by Ringler in *A Midsummer Night's Dream*, takes its particular play one step further in that play's own direction.

Consider the effects on two plays that dwell on the inconclusiveness of murder if the actor murdered as Julius Caesar returns not only as Caesar's ghost in IV.iii but also as his nephew Octavius in IV.i and V.i, and if the actor murdered as Duncan does indeed wake Duncan with his knocking by returning as Macduff to discover his own body.[7] And, again in *Macbeth,* consider the thematic underscoring available to the text from a production that doubled the tiny roles of Fleance, the second apparition (a bloody child), and/or the third apparition (a crowned child with a tree in his hand), one or both of the "cream-faced loon" (who brings Macbeth news of the English force in V.iii) and the messenger in V.v (who informs Macbeth that Birnam Wood is marching toward Dunsinane), and, perhaps, Donalbain and young Siward. The experience of *Macbeth* is also enriched if the men who play the two murderers in III.i play witches in earlier and later scenes: if, when the unexpected third murderer joins them for the attack on Banquo and Fleance in III.iii, the actor who plays the third murderer is the same man who elsewhere plays the third witch, then a character whose presence is justly called gratuitous to the situation (III.iii.1−4) is in another dimension—that of the particular production—the extranarratively pertinent missing third in a well established trio of actors. Banquo's perseverence—otherwise established in two dimensions (he rises as a ghost and, through Fleance, lives forever in his descendents)—is reasserted in any production where the actor who plays Banquo returns as Old Siward.

Consider the quite differently ironic effect if in II.i of *Richard II* the scrupulous Gaunt is helped off the stage at line 138 and the same actor returns at line 146 in the person of the unscrupulous Northumberland, Bolingbroke's political foster father, to announce Gaunt's death:

> *Northumberland.* My liege, old Gaunt commends him to your majesty.
> *King.* What says he?
> *Northumberland.* Nay, nothing; all is said.
>   His tongue is now a stringless instrument;
>   Words, life, and all, old Lancaster hath spent.
>
> [147–50]

Northumberland next speaks seventy lines later, when he and his fellow conspirators are left alone on the stage:

> *Northumberland.* Well, lords, the Duke of Lancaster is dead.
> *Ross.* And living too; for now his son is duke.
>
> [224–25]

In both *Henry IV* and *2 Henry IV* Poins vanishes after II.iv; Prince John arrives late in both plays (in V.i of Part One, in IV.ii of Part Two). If one actor played both roles, that fact of production would amplify likenesses and contrasts between the two characters. Both Poins and Prince John are young men specifically and regularly compared to Hal. Each of the two is disadvantaged by being a younger son. They are also alike in thinking up tricks: Poins conceives the comic disguise plots against Falstaff at Gadshill in Part I and at the tavern in Part II: Prince John's trick at Gaultree in Part II is similarly clever and dissimilarly seriously in its intent and consequences.

A heightening of relationship already embodied in the text would result from doubling Rumor—the prologue of *2 Henry IV*—with Pistol: Rumor, "painted full of tongues" and concerned with the power of hollow words, is echoed in Pistol, who is all talk and who at the end of the play brings Falstaff the accurate news that Hal is now king and the inaccurate news that Falstaff is "now one of the greatest men in this realm" (V.iii. 85–86). (Note the lines about winds and news with which Falstaff and Pistol greet each other in V.iii [83–94]; they echo the language of the first half of Rumor's speech.)

In the same play, the actor who played Northumberland—old, ineffectual, confused, and isolated—could have underscored the likeness between Northumberland (who is last seen in II.iii) and old, ineffectual, confused, isolated Shallow (who first appears in III.ii), or old, ineffectual, confused, isolated Henry IV (who first appears in III.i), by playing one or the other of those parts. The three grooms who speak one sentence each at the beginning of the last scene of *2 Henry IV*, the rejection scene, serve no necessary expository function (the job of scene setting they do becomes immediately redundant). They seem to be in the play only to establish the scene as an echo of II.iv, the big tavern scene—a scene that also begins with three servants who, like the three grooms, await Prince Hal's arrival in an altered guise in which he will surprise Falstaff. To double the actors who played Francis and the other two drawers in II.iv as the three grooms in the last scene would be to accentuate a parallel that the text itself goes out of its way to point up.

In *Romeo and Juliet* Shakespeare belatedly labels Mercutio and Paris as "a brace of kinsmen" to Prince Escalus (V.iii.294–95). The carnage among the prince's relatives demonstrates that the woe said to be generated by the feud extends to a family of bystanders innocent of even blood ties to the Montagues and Capulets. However, the family relationship among Escalus, Mercutio, and Paris is so haphazardly and casually established within the fiction, that it may have been registered only as the formal incorporation of a link already obvious to an audience that saw all three played by one actor.[8]

Dolabella, Cleopatra's last conquest and the character addressed in the last sentence of *Antony and Cleopatra,* first appears at the beginning of III.xii—a scene to which he is not obviously necessary. Dolabella's one speech in that scene is spoken in answer to its first speech—Caesar's "Let him appear that's come from Antony. / Know you him?"—and is spoken by a character new to us and left unidentified for the whole length of the scene (Dolabella is not named until V.i). The speech derives from Plutarch, who says that at the time of this embassy Antony and Cleopatra, "because they had no other men of estimation about them, for that some were fled, and, those that remained, they did not greatly trust them: they were enforced to send Euphronius the schoolmaster of their children" (*Four Lives from North's Plutarch,* ed. R. H. Carr [Oxford, 1906], p. 232):

Caesar, 'tis his schoolmaster:
An argument that he is plucked, when hither

He sends so poor a pinion of his wing,
Which had superfluous kings for messengers
Not many moons gone by.

[III.xii.2−6]

Shakespeare introduces Dolabella, who, though listed as present in IV.vi, will not speak again until V.i, into the play at an unnecessarily early point (Agrippa or Thidias could easily have spoken the speech identifying the ambassador)—introduces him *only* to deal with a question of identity and to speak a scornful speech on the topic of Antony's lack of manpower.

In the first line of V.i, Caesar sends Dolabella to treat with Antony ("Go to him, Dolabella, bid him yield"). Then Decretas enters to report Antony's death to Caesar. The dying Antony gave Cleopatra one piece of specific advice: "None about Caesar trust but Proculeius" (IV.xv.48). The scene that began with Dolabella's embassy to Antony ends with the introduction of Proculeius (who might profitably have been played by the actor who previously played Enobarbus); Caesar sends Proculeius on a mission to Cleopatra, a mission parallel to Dolabella's to Antony:

Caesar. Come hither, Proculeius. Go and say
    We purpose her no shame: give her what comforts
    The quality of her passion shall require,
    Lest, in her greatness, by some mortal stroke
    She do defeat us. For her life in Rome
    Would be eternal in our triumph. Go,
    And with your speediest bring us what she says
    And how you find of her.
Proculeius.   Caesar, I shall.   *Exit.*
Caesar. Gallus, go you along. [*Exit Gallus.*] Where's Dolabella,
    To second Proculeius?
All.   Dolabella!
Caesar. Let him alone, for I remember now
    How he's employed. He shall in time be ready. . . .

[V.i.61−72]

Caesar's lapse of memory seems gratuitous at best; all it does is emphasize the parellel between Proculeius and Dolabella, remind us that Dolabella's employment is a mission to a dead man, and give Dolabella special prominence.

In the next scene, the last of the play, Proculeius immediately demonstrates the error of Antony's trust by objectifying the perfidy inherent in the instructions we have just heard Caesar give. After Proculeius has tricked and captured Cleopatra, Dolabella, the one man about Caesar who turns out to warrant Cleopatra's trust, enters and takes charge of the prisoner. When he and Cleopatra are alone, Dolabella's first concern is with his own identity. That concern reemphasizes the parallel between himself and Proculeius (whose interview Cleopatra began by asking his name). Dolabella, however, stresses his identity with an intensity that seems curious but would be justified and dramatically powerful if the actor we saw in our own dream of an Antony were now before us as Dolabella. The doubling of the parts would also give a special falsehood and a more special truth to "Gentle madam, no":

Dolabella. Most noble Empress, you have heard of me?
Cleopatra. I cannot tell.
Dolabella. Assuredly you know me.
Cleopatra. No matter, sir, what I have heard or known.
　　You laugh when boys or women tell their dreams;
　　Is't not your trick?
Dolabella. 　　　　　　I understand not, madam.
Cleopatra. I dreamt there was an Emperor Antony.
　　O, such another sleep, that I might see
　　But such another man.
Dolabella. 　　　　　　If it might please ye—
Cleopatra. His face was as the heav'ns, and therein stuck
　　A sun and moon, which kept their course and lighted
　　The little O, th' earth.
Dolabella. 　　　　　　Most sovereign creature—
Cleopatra. His legs bestrid the ocean . . .
. . . .
　　. . . realms and islands were
　　As plates dropped from his pocket.
Dolabella. 　　　　　　Cleopatra—
Cleopatra. Think you there was or might be such a man
　　As this I dreamt of?
Dolabella. 　　　　　Gentle madam, no.
　　　　　　　　　　　　　　　　[71–82, 91–94]

(Note that "boys or women" and "The little O, th' earth" might remind an audience that it is itself surrendering to a dream—that it is in a theatre called The Globe listening to a boy dressed up as the Queen of Egypt.)

In the great restitution at the end of *The Winter's Tale* two losses are
irrevocable: Mamilius and Antigonus are dead and gone. I suspect
that, although they are not restored in one dimension of the play, its
story, they were restored in a second dimension, the performance.
Mamilius's death was reported in III.ii:

> *Servant.* . . . The prince your son, with mere conceit and fear
>   O the queen's speed, is gone.
> *Leontes.*   How? gone?
> *Servant.*   Is dead.
>
>   [142–43]

In the final scene Mamilius is all but forgotten. Two scenes earlier,
when the fugitive Florizel and Perdita are about to be brought before
Leontes, Paulina brings up Mamilius:

> *Paulina.*   Had our prince,
>   Jewel of children, seen this hour, he had paired
>   Well with this lord. There was not full a month
>   Between their births.
> *Leontes.*   Prithee, no more; cease. Thou know'st
>   He dies to me again when talked of. Sure,
>   When I shall see this gentleman [Florizel], thy speeches
>   Will bring me to consider that which may
>   Unfurnish me of reason.
>
>   [V.i.115–22]

Mamilius remains a recurring topic for the rest of the scene. For
instance, Florizel and Perdita enter during Leontes's response to
Paulina, and Leontes immediately addresses Florizel in words that
echo lines spoken earlier to and about Mamilius and Perdita:

> Your mother was most true to wedlock, prince,
> For she did print your royal father off,
> Conceiving you.
>
>   [123–25]

The ensuing dialogue is too rich a jumble of real, feigned, assumed, past, present, and potential identities to describe here—and
is too long to quote. Suffice it to say that, if the actor who played
Mamilius were now playing Perdita, the jumble would be sufficient
nearly to unfurnish an audience of reason. *If* the actor who played
Mamilius also played Perdita, then, when Leontes said, "What might
I have been, / Might I a son and daughter now have looked on, /

Such goodly things as you" (175—77), he would have been doing so in three very different ways: Perdita is the daughter he thinks dead; Florizel, "paired well with" Perdita rather than Mamilius, will be Leontes's son by marriage; and this seeming lady, the boy actor dressed as Perdita the shepherdess, would—in *theatrical* fact—be Leontes's lost son Mamilius. Such intercourse between fictional and theatrical reality could make Mamilius's subsequent fall from the characters' memory more palatable.

Antigonus is not forgotton. At the very end, after everyone else has been brought to a fairy-tale prospect, Paulina says:

> Go together,
> You precious winners all; your exultation
> Partake to every one. I, an old turtle,
> Will wing me to some withered bough and there
> My mate, that's never to be found again,
> Lament till I am lost.
>
> [V.iii.130—35]

Thereupon, in the last speech of the play, Leontes suddenly makes dramatically impromptu restitution for Paulina's loss:

> O, peace Paulina!
> Thou shouldst a husband take by my consent,
> As I by thine a wife. This is a match,
> And made between's by vows. Thou hast found mine;
> But how, is to be questioned, for I saw her,
> As I thought, dead, and have in vain said many
> A prayer upon her grave. I'll not seek far—
> For him, I partly know his mind—to find thee
> An honourable husband. Come, Camillo,
> And take her by the hand, whose worth and honesty
> Is richly noted and here justified
> By us, a pair of kings. . . .
>
> [135—46]

Five lines later Leontes concludes the play with a specifically theatrical metaphor:

> Good Paulina,
> Lead us from hence, where we may leisurely
> Each one demand and answer to his part
> Performed in this wide gap of time since first

We were dissevered. Hastily lead away.

[151-55]

The pairing of Paulina and Camillo (whose function as Leontes's chief courtier is taken on by Antigonus after Act I) would have seemed less arbitrary, less an act of mere authorial tidiness, to an audience that saw one actor play Antigonus in Acts II and III and Camillo in the other three acts. Such an audience would have seen the story line of this winter's tale, this old wives' tale, conclude with Leontes getting his old wife back and the theatrical event conclude with Paulina getting her old husband back.[9]

In *Twelfth Night,* Maria is the only major character who fails to appear in the final scene. The reason may be that the actor who played Maria was onstage in another character. It is tempting to think about the dramatic implications if Maria (whose handwriting is nearly indistinguishable from Olivia's, and who is thus a mainspring of one plot line) and Sebastian (whose likeness to Viola powers another) were in *fact* indistinguishable in the reality superseded by the temporary identities it is an actor's profession to assume. The entrances and exits of Maria and Sebastian in III.ii, iii, and iv require them to trip over each other in the wings, but those scenes comment on one another, and—given producers and audiences attuned to conventions other than ours—the doubling would give the themes of *Twelfth Night* an appropriate extra dimension and extend them into the actual experience of the audience.

Twelfth Night could be described as a collection of variations on the word *suit*. Although the characters take no note of Maria's absence from the last scene, they do have need of the sea captain who rescued Viola. He appears only in I.ii—where he performs a necessary and demanding task of exposition by laying out all the givens of Illyrian society, and where Viola's suggestion that she become a follower of Olivia leads into this exchange:

Viola.   O that I served that lady,
  And might not be delivered to the world,
  Till I had made mine own occasion mellow,
  What my estate is.
Captain.   That were hard to compass,

> Because she will admit no kind of suit,
> No, not the Duke's.
> *Viola.* There is a fair behavior in thee, captain,
> And though that nature with a beauteous wall
> Doth oft close in pollution, yet of thee
> I will believe thou hast a mind that suits
> With this thy fair and outward character.
> I prithee (and I'll pay thee bounteously)
> Conceal me what I am, and be my aid
> For such disguise as haply shall become
> The form of my intent. I'll serve this duke. . . .
> *Captain.* Be you his eunuch, and your mute I'll be;
> When my tongue blabs, then let mine eyes not see.
> *Viola.* I thank thee. Lead me on.
>
> [41–55, 62–64]

In the last scene, when occasion is so mellow that only Malvolio's problem remains to be solved and nothing lets to make the lovers happy except Viola's "masculine usurped attire," she says this:

> The captain that did bring me first on shore
> Hath my maid's garments. He upon some action
> Is now in durance, at Malvolio's suit,
> A gentleman, and follower of my lady's.
>
> [V.i.266–69]

What if Shakespeare wrote both parts for one actor who wore one suit as the captain in I.ii and thereafter changed his clothes to become Malvolio (whose tongue blabs, who changes his clothes as the letter instructs him, and who is bound in a dark room)?

Curiously enough, *Love's Labor's Lost*—a play in which the issue of doubling parts (in the pageant of Worthies) is an issue for the characters, and a play in which every major character but Jaquenetta, Boyet, and Dull goes into disguise at some point (Holofernes, Armado, Nathaniel, Moth, and Costard perform as Worthies; the four young men dress up as Russians; and the four ladies disguise themselves as one another)—leaves very little room for the sort of rhetorically rewarding doubling I propose here.

Jaquenetta, however, is an exception. On the modern stage, where, of course, roles are ordinarily doubled only from necessity, one of the actresses playing Maria or Katherine would be the probable choice if someone had to double as Jaquenetta. If my theory is correct, the original double could profitably have been Rosaline-Jaquenetta. Berowne, whose letter to Rosaline gets exchanged for Armado's letter to Jaquenetta, insists, like Armado, on the unworthiness of his beloved, and doubling Rosaline and Jaquenetta would underscore the persistent, play-long comparison of Rosaline's suitor with Costard and Armado, Jaquenetta's suitors.

Like Jaquenetta, Constable Dull does not do any playacting in the course of the plot of *Love's Labor's Lost*—although he does promise to "make one in a dance" and "play on the tabor to the Worthies, and let them dance the hay" (V.i.139—40). Such dancing would customarily have followed the pageant—which is interrupted and never reaches conclusion. A purely poetic justice could have been achieved from doubling Dull (who at I.i.178 is the first intruding messenger to disrupt a frail, arbitrary norm in *Love's Labor's Lost*) and Marcade (the last).

Cymbeline begins with two gentlemen who furnish exposition that establishes the thematic and narrative bases for the play. The two gentlemen are interchangeable in all respects save that the first has information for which the second catechizes him. Throughout their seventy-line conversation they insist on, inquire about, assert, attempt to establish, and inadvertently dissolve various kinds of *uniqueness*—a concept always at the surface of their talk and also embedded, either positively or negatively, in their syntax ("You do not meet a man but frowns"—I.i.1) and diction ("his wife's sole son," "None but the King," "Is she sole child to th' King?"—5, 10, 56).

Above all, the first gentleman insists that Posthumus is uniquely superior to all other men; but at the passionate height of his admiration he introduces (47—50) the altogether appropriate and altogether subversive notion of Posthumus as, in Ophelia's terms, "the glass of fashion." Not surprisingly, the first gentleman's insistence on the difference between Posthumus and all other creatures relies heavily both on assertions that Posthumus is beyond compare and on comparisons between him and other men—notably Cloten, his fellow foster-child to Cymbeline and his rival for Imogen. Consider this passage, which delivers its sense perfectly straightforwardly but is variously confusing, confused, and self-defeating in its structure:

He that hath missed the Princess is a thing
Too bad for bad report, and he that hath her—
I mean, that married her, alack good man,
And therefore banished—is a creature such
As, to seek through the regions of the earth
For one his like, there would be something failing
In him that should compare. I do not think
So fair an outward and such stuff within
Endows a man but he.

                                        [16—24]

There are intriguing—but, of course, by no means definitive —signs that *Cymbeline* was written with the expectation that the substantively accidental facts of its performance would supplement, and provide a harmonious running commentary on, the themes, ironies, and texture of the play.

Since the most spectacular double would be Posthumus/Cloten, consider the nonspectacular matter of the doubtful departure of the banished Posthumus. In his first substantial speech, the first gentleman invites us to assume that Posthumus has already left Britain ("[Imogen is] wedded, / Her husband banished, she imprisoned"—"7—8); but Posthumus and Imogen enter with the Queen at I.i.70 (I.ii.1 in modern editions that follow the Folio's scene division). Both women urge Posthumus to depart quickly, and sixty lines later, Posthumus does in fact set out for Rome. Thirty lines after he exits we hear that, within moments of Posthumus's departure from the stage, Cloten met and challenged him, and that the two have for the last few minutes been fighting just offstage from the place where Imogen bade Posthumus farewell, the place where she has remained to lament their parting. Then, after a conversation among Imogen, the Queen, and Pisanio about Cloten and Posthumus (a conversation that includes Imogen's deeply ambiguous "I would they were in Afric both together, / Myself by with a needle, that I might prick / The goer-back"—167—69 [Folio, I.ii.97—99]), the stage clears, and Cloten makes his first entrance—with two lords, the first of whom opens the scene (I.ii or Folio, I.iii) by saying "Sir, I would advise you to shift a shirt." If the actor who, as Posthumus, has finally departed from Britain has now changed his costume and remains to play his rival, then the first lord's suggestion takes on an extra dimension that does not intrude upon the fiction but does complement it.

There is neither space here nor probable need to rehearse the events of *Cymbeline* in order to demonstrate that the play lends itself to production with one actor in the insistently contrasted roles of Posthumus and Cloten—or to spell out the various ways in which that production device would lend something appropriate and positive to the play. A few reminders should be enough: *Cymbeline* dwells persistently on the frailty of eyesight, on the frailty of judgment, on the ricketiness of all evidence, and on the limited capacity of clothing to transform its wearer or deceive those who see him. The parallel between the invaluable Posthumus and the worthless Cloten culminates in IV.ii when Imogen awakens beside the headless corpse of Cloten and recognizes it as Posthumus—not only by its borrowed clothing but by "the shape of's leg . . . his hand, / His foot Mercurial, his Martial thigh" (309–10), and so on. Imogen's error is echoed in the last scene of the play when Posthumus fails to recognize Imogen and throws her violently aside as he abuses her in a sustained theatrical metaphor: "Shall's have a play of this? Thou scornful page, / There lie thy part" (V.v.228–29).

Instead of laboring a case for doubling Posthumus and Cloten, I want to return to the two gentlemen in scene i to offer token support for the more complex and less immediately interesting proposition that the fusion and confusion of absolutely distinguishable identities is so of the essence of *Cymbeline* and of an audience's experience of its smallest details that the grosser manifestation in theatrical doubling is all but an aesthetic inevitability.

The gentlemen's opening conversation, concerned as it is for absolutes, dwells on two major examples of contrasting but confusable pairs in addition to Posthumus and Cloten, pairs that get confused in and by the gentlemen's syntax and diction: appearance as opposed to inward truth (I.i.1–3, 9–14, 22–25), and the family of Sicilius Leonatus (of whose three children only one survives) as opposed to that of Cymbeline (of whose three children only one is known to survive). The three major contrasts coexist with and overlap with several incidental pairs (Cloten is the Queen's "sole son," and Imogen is "sole child to th' King; the Queen and Imogen—among others —nearly become confused in lines 4–7: "His daughter, and the heir of's kingdom, whom / He purposed to his wife's sole son—a widow / That late he married—hath referred herself / Unto a poor but worthy gentleman. She's wedded . . ."; and so on).

Of these incidental confusions the most incidental, most complicated, and most emblematic occur in the following lines on
Posthumus's "name and birth"; the passage focuses on names—and is
so precise in its details that its distinctions become indistinct:

> I cannot delve him to the root. His father
> Was called Sicilius, who did join his honor
> Against the Romans with Cassibelan,
> But had his titles by Tenantius, whom
> He served with glory and admired success,
> So gained the sur-addition Leonatus . . .

[28−33]

The syntactic and ideational physics of the subordinate clause mod-
ifying "Sicilius" present Cymbeline's two royal predecessors in such
a way as to make the pairing feel like a contrast and—illogically
—to imply an opposition between them—an opposition that the
clause does not in fact assert: consider the fleeting false signals inherent in the mere presence of *Against,* the inversion of the unambigu-
ous, normal sentence structure (which would be "did join his honor
with Cassibelan against the Romans"), and the implications of rever-
sal and of Tenantius as the reverser in the use of *by* (the words *But* and
by here beckon the listening mind toward some such conclusion as
"But had his titles by Tenantius revoked"). Similarly, almost as
incidentally, but even more complexly, Posthumus's father is named
to us in a way that minimizes the definition naming is designed to
provide. Posthumus's father "was called Sicilius" ("was" is a simple
preterite, appropriate because—and indicating that—Sicilius is dead);
but Sicilius later "gained the sur-addition Leonatus" (so *was*, now five
lines in the past, acquires a syntactically posthumus addition, the
sense "was originally").[10]

Confusion by means of names—by means of labels that fix identity—continues into the next generation and thus into the body of
the play: Posthumus Leonatus is sometimes called Posthumus, sometimes Leonatus; and an audience has slight but constant difficulty
jumping from one label to another. A variation on the phenomenon
occurs on a larger scale in Imogen-Fidele and in Guiderius-Polydore,
Arviragus-Cadwal, and Belarius-Morgan. Finally—in the prophecy that is miraculously delivered to Posthumus during his dream
(V.iv.138−44)[11] and is later read again and interpreted by the sooth-

sayer (V.v.435−57)—the play-long network of labels that fail to define because they overdo their specificity flowers luxuriously into the clarifying confusions of a series of overlapping puns and arch etymologies: "piece"—*woman*, "piece"—"branches," "piece"— "peace," "tender air"—*tender heir*, "Leonatus"—"Lion's whelp," "lopped"—"clipped about," "piece of tender air"—"mollis aer"— "mulier."

The list of possibilities for doubling is long and tempting.[12] For instance, I have said nothing about the thematic expansion that could result from doubling Egeon and Dr. Pinch in *The Comedy of Errors* (see V.i.294), or about the pertinent mental extravagance to be had from doubling Desdemona (Othello's innocent but falsely slandered white wife) and the urgently named Bianca (the white—the hoar—whore). But I will do well to return to *King Lear,* where the grounds for speculation are at least relatively firm.

Nahum Tate's sense that by all the laws of fiction Cordelia and Edgar are meant to marry might once have been fulfilled outside the fiction in what the audience actually saw on the stage; the actor who played the King of France in scene i may have played Edgar there-after—thereby making a sort of "in" joke of onstage puzzlement about Cordelia's husband's unexpected return to France before the battle at Dover:

> *Kent.* Why the King of France is so suddenly gone back
>   know you no reason?
> *Gentleman.* Something he left imperfect in the state,
>   which since his coming forth is thought of, which
>   imports to the kingdom so much fear and danger
>   that his personal return was most required and
>   necessary.
>
>   [IV.iii.1−6]

Doubling of parts would also have added dimension to the "cloth-ing" theme in *Lear*.

But the intriguing topic remains Cordelia and the Fool.

From the beginning of the play to the end, Shakespeare emphasizes the parallel between Kent and Edgar and between Cordelia and both. In scene i Lear's rejection of his blunt-spoken daughter is intertwined with his rejection of the blunt-spoken Kent, who says he loved Lear as he would a father (I.i.141). The likeness between Lear's wronged child and Gloucester's is obvious and directly stated several times. In the last scene, the parallel between Edgar and Kent is underscored when we hear that they have exchanged accounts of their activities in disguise (V.iii.209–16). The pairing of Kent and Cordelia recurs in the lines over Cordelia's body, where alternation between certainty that Caius is dead and certainty that he is living interrupts Lear's series of similar alternations about Cordelia's state. In complement to the paired banishments of Kent and Cordelia in scene i, the introduction of the disguised Kent in scene iv flows into and fuses with Lear's call for the Fool. The first specific information we get about the Fool not only links him with Cordelia but presents the Fool's condition as contingent on the presence or absence of Cordelia (in the following passage, note the general confusion about who is who, who is being sent for, and who answers):

> *Lear.* . . . But where's my fool? I have not seen
> him this two days.
> *Knight.* Since my young lady's going into France, sir,
> the fool hath much pined away.
> *Lear.* No more of that; I have noted it well. Go you
> and tell my daughter I would speak with her.
> [*Exit Knight.*]
> Go you, call hither my fool. [*Exit an Attendant.*]
>   *Enter Steward* [*Oswald*].
> O, you, sir, you! Come you hither, sir. Who am I, sir?
> *Oswald.* My lady's father.
> *Lear.* 'My lady's father'? My lord's knave, you whoreson
> dog, you slave, you cur!
>
> [I.iv.68–78]

Kent and Edgar spend the body of the play succoring Lear and Gloucester. Each is disguised, and each is disguised as a kind of fool (Edgar as mad Tom; Kent as Caius, who sounds like, and whom Lear treats like, a professional clown—see I.iv.9–43, 90).

Cordelia leaves England for France, leaves Lear, leaves the play; but, though the character goes, the actor may have stayed behind to maintain the parallel between Cordelia and the two victims who disguise themselves to provide kind nursery for their erring oppressors.

I should say one more time that this essay does not pretend to add to our knowledge of Renaissance stage practices. At most it questions some assumptions by which our thinking has been arbitrarily bound and offers some directions in which informed ignorance may justly but tentatively range.[13]

There could, however, be some solid, practical use to this essay if it were to encourage modern directors to follow Brook in exploiting the theatrical energy inherent in the doubling of parts by companies that revel in the practice and, like their audiences, revel in the theatricality of theatre. We might also get more productions of *Cymbeline* if it were taken to contain two star turns—not only Imogen but Posthumus / Cloten; and we might get better productions of *As You Like It* if a producer could lure a first-class character actor into the double role of the two dukes by means of a single, and therefore large, salary and the temptations of a professionally rewarding theatrical vehicle.

NOTES

Part I

1 *Johnson on Shakespeare,* ed. Arthur Sherbo, 2 vols., vols. 7 and 8 of the Yale Edition of the Works of Samuel Johnson (New Haven, 1968), 8: 704. Subsequent quotations from Johnson are also from Sherbo's text.
2 Although the independent integrity of the Quarto and Folio texts of *King Lear* has been established by the work of Michael J. Warren ("Quarto and Folio *King Lear,* and the Interpretation of Albany and Edgar," in David Bevington and Jay L. Halio, eds., *Shakespeare: Pattern of Excelling Nature* [Newark, Del., 1978], pp. 95–107), Steven Urkowitz (*Shakespeare's Revision of King Lear* [Princeton, 1980]), and Gary Taylor ("The War in *King Lear,*" *Shakespeare Survey* 33 [1980], 27–34), all my references to *King Lear* are to Alfred Harbage's Revised Pelican Text of 1969. This discussion, thus, is based on the traditional, now familiar *King Lear* of modern editions—a *King Lear* editorially derived, usually, as in the Pelican, by supplementing the Folio text with lines from the Quarto. In basing my essay on Harbage's conservative conflation, I am not merely being old-fashioned or merely being lazy. Unfortunately, the altogether persuasive demonstrations by Warren, Urkowitz, and Taylor cannot imply a corollary by which one simply uses the Folio *Lear* (or, less reasonably, the Quarto *Lear*).

Granting that we have in the past been foolishly presumptive about the originals that lie behind the seventeenth-century printed texts, both those texts *are* faulty. The Folio text of *Lear* is, like the more blatantly corrupt Quarto, obviously deficient—not only deficient when measured against some hypothetical Platonic original dimly visible in a conflation of the two versions, but deficient in its own terms. For example, in the Folio text of I.iv, Lear asks the Fool to teach him the difference between a bitter fool and a sweet one, but the Fool's lesson is missing: as reported in the Folio, the Fool's response is "Nuncle, give me an egg, and I'll give thee two crowns." And there is no logic to *Then* in Lear's "Then let them anatomize Regan" in the Folio text of III.vi where no arraignment of Goneril precedes it.

The traditional editor-made conflation can no longer be assumed to approximate Shakespeare's intent, but—as a practical text for criticism—the conflation appears to come closer to doing so than either of the more authoritative texts that provide its raw material. Even after scholarly texts of Q and F are readily available, our idea of the two "real" *King Lear*s will presumably be comparable to our now discarded idea of the mythical single lost one: we will still be dependent on editor-made texts for performances of either of the two *Lear*s and on heavily and speculatively annotated texts for reading them.

Moreover—and more importantly—my topic in this essay is in *fact* neither of Shakespeare's *King Lear*s but the *King Lear* familiar to students of the play and, at least in this century, familiar to playgoers for whom ad hoc abbreviations of the edited conflation are played. This essay—an essay not on the greatness of Shakespeare but on the greatness of *King Lear*—is concerned with the *King Lear* in which, throughout the history of modern scholarship, that greatness has been perceived (and which remains great, no matter how it came into being). I am, in short, concerned here with our *King Lear*—shaped though it is by accidents and editors—rather than either of Shakespeare's.

This whole matter of the texts of *Lear* is philosophically vexing and will remain so. Fortunately, however, my thesis in this essay is not materially dependent on my choice of text. That, I believe, is true—even though, since I make an issue of the extreme length of *King Lear,* and since editorially conflated texts are about a hundred lines longer than the Q text and almost three hundred lines longer than the F text, my thesis could seem to depend very materially indeed upon my decision to use the Pelican text. In fact, because my concern is not with the literal duration of the play—how long it takes to say out all its lines—but with how long the play *feels,* the addition or subtraction of a hundred or even three hundred lines does not much affect my argument. The F text, the Q text, and modern conflations all seem unbearably long, and seem so for reasons essentially unrelated to the actual length of the play.

3 *King Lear* is now so famous that even people seeing or reading it for the first time know a lot about it. The mere fact that we know—if only from the categorical title the play received in the 1623 Folio—that this is *The Tragedie of King Lear* is by itself enough to tell a modern audience more about "the promised end" of *King Lear* than my discussion allows for. More importantly, my discussion makes no allowance whatever for distinctions between first impressions of *King Lear* and the responses of audiences and readers who see or read the play for the second, third, fourth, fifth . . . time. The issue is vital and complex—so complex as to warrant a digression that would make an unreasonably awkward bulge in the discussion that occasions it. I therefor reserve it for an appendix: Appendix 1, "On the Persistence of First Impressions," pp. 119–25 below.

4 Compare the similarly circumscribed field of possibility assumed in Edmund's "The younger rises when the old doth fall" (III.iii.23). For

other specific references to Fortune's wheel, see the last speech of II. ii and V.iii.175. Also note V.iii.5–6 and the Fool's "Fortune, that arrant whore, / Ne'er turns the key to th' poor" (II.iv.50–51), where "turns," which relates to "Fortune" in one available ideational set (Fortune's wheel) and to *whore* in another ("to turn" was slang for "to copulate"), comes finally to function exclusively in a metaphor of locks and turning keys, a metaphor related to fortune (wealth), unrelated to the goddess Fortuna, but traditionally associated with brothel-keeping (see *Othello* IV.ii.91–94).

5 A similar dimness of distinction between Lear and God occurs in IV.iv.23–24, when Cordelia says, "O dear father, / It is thy business that I go about"—an echo of Christ's words in Luke 2 : 49: "knewe ye not that I must go about my fathers busines?" (Geneva text, 1560).

6 See *As You Like It,* I.ii.106–07 where Celia jokes about the generic assurances inherent in fictional situations:

> *Le Beau.* There comes an old man and his three sons.
> *Celia.* I could match this beginning with an old tale.

In "The Multiple Genres of *King Lear:* Breaking the Archetypes" (*Bucknell Review* 16 [1968]: 40–63)—a valuable essay that treats many of the phenomena I treat here—Katherine Stockholder comments usefully on the fairy-tale elements in *King Lear* and on the twists Shakespeare gives to the expectations the genre raises. She observes that the first scene of *Lear* "no sooner arouses an expectation of a far-off happy ending than it unexpectedly satisfies it. Cordelia finds her unaccommodated excellence appreciated by France, and leaves with him. . . . The conventional fairy tale would have the two evil sisters either dead or repentant, in any case powerless, by the time Cordelia achieved her happiness. As it is, the fairy tale [i.e., the fairy tale of Cordelia—the tale told with the virtuous youngest daughter as its focus, not the mistaken father] ends when the play has scarcely begun . . ." (pp. 44–45).

7 Lear never does, however, enter the promised hovel. The place for which the characters depart at the end of III.iv and in which they find brief shelter in III.vi is the never precisely located place offered by Gloucester in III.iv.139–44:

> Go in with me. My duty cannot suffer
> T'obey in all your daughters' hard commands.
> Though their injunction be to bar my doors
> And let this tyrannous night take hold upon you,
> Yet have I ventured to come seek you out
> And bring you where both fire and food is ready.

8 The *idea* that *King Lear* has a moral—reveals some general and portable truth to us—is a fact of the play, is "in" it as much as any other of the responses the play regularly evokes.

Although I insist that Lear learns nothing in the course of the play and that *King Lear* has nothing to teach us, I also insist that the sense that Lear learns and that the play illuminates is *of* the play — is generated by *King Lear,* not foisted upon it by the benignly creative commentators who insist on telling us *what* Lear learns and *what* the great human truths are that *King Lear* so evidently makes evident. The fact that we find *Lear* "meaningful" leads us to try to identify the meanings that fill it. The fact that we cannot find the meaning or meanings we seek does not, however, deny the fact that sends us questing: *King Lear* feels profoundly illuminating. The play does not reveal the true nature of things, but it does—or seems to—prove that nature can *be* revealed and is contained within *King Lear,* a play whose glow assures us that within its humanly manageable compass is the light by which to see the essential truth of the human condition. An audience to *King Lear* does not see the light but knows itself to be where light is.

9 Shakespeare makes similarly (but significantly) unobtrusive use of contrasting metaphoric connotations of stone in *Julius Caesar,* a play in which his audience is persistently urged to feel contempt for the mob's ridiculously indiscriminate openness to rhetorical gestures, in which that audience accepts "You blocks, you stones, you worse than senseless things" (I.i.35) as fitting epithets for a mob so insensitive to reason that its sympathies wander in response to any idle stimulus, and in which that same audience accepts the mob's *un*likeness to the same objects as evidence of the same set of qualities: "You are not wood, you are not stones, but men" (III.ii.142).

10 *Essays in Criticism* 16 (1966): 262–64. Shaw also remarks another patterning effect in which Albany's speech participates: "Albany's speech stands in neat and symmetrical relationship to Lear's first speech of the play. In that speech Lear had spoken of his 'fast intent' to abdicate, and Albany, repeating the very phrase, speaks of 'our intent' to 'resign . . . our absolute power' " (p. 265).

11 In particular, note "where is your servant Caius?" (284). This is the first and only time Kent's alias is mentioned; at the moment we hear Kent's question, the name is meaningless to us, and the question is therefore an intrusive irrelevancy in our real experience—our experience of watching and hearing the play.

12 Compare Shallow's nostalgic boast in *Merry Wives of Windsor* II.i.202–03: "I have seen the time with my long sword I would have made you four tall fellows skip like rats," and York's in *Richard II,* II.iii.99–105:

> Were I but now lord of such hot youth
> As when brave Gaunt thy father and myself
> Rescued the Black Prince, that young Mars of men,
> From forth the ranks of many thousand French,
> O, then how quickly should this arm of mine,
> Now prisoner to the palsy, chastise thee
> And minister correction to thy fault!

Also note *Much Ado about Nothing,* V.i.58–62, the lines with which Leonato prefaces his challenge to Claudio:

> Tush, tush, man! never fleer and jest at me.
> I speak not like a dotard nor a fool,
> As under privilege of age to brag
> What I have done being young, or what would do,
> Were I not old.

13 Although our emphases differ, Arthur M. Eastman has already said most of what I say about "And my poor fool is hanged" in a splendidly sensible essay called "King Lear's 'Poor Fool' " (*Papers of the Michigan Academy of Science, Arts and Letters* 49 [1964]: 531–40).

14 Note that "And my poor fool is hanged" resembles the Fool's own last line in the play, III.vi.83, a line that plays openly with the capacity of the word *and* to introduce a non sequitur: "And I'll go to bed at noon."

15 See Appendix 2, "Speculations on Doubling in Shakespeare's Plays"; in particular, see pp. 129 and 153–54. If the roles of the Fool and Cordelia were indeed played by a single actor, the doubling of those two parts in performance would give another dimension of unsteadiness to the Fool's identity.

16 Some landmarks for this sort of documentatioı are "Gloucester's Eyes" by P. V. Kreider (*SAB* 8 [1933]: 121–32), R. B. Heilman's distinguished, vastly influential *This Great Stage: Image and Structure in Lear* (Baton Rouge, La., 1948), Donald Stauffer's *Shakespeare's World of Images* (New York, 1949), J. F. Danby's *Shakespeare's Doctrine of Nature: A Study of King Lear* (London, 1949), and William Empson's " 'Fool' in *Lear*" in *The Structures of Complex Words* (London and Norfolk, Conn., 1951).

17 For an example of the lunatic limitlessness I will discuss below, see I.i.277–78: "your lord, who hath received you / At fortune's alms"; through the intermediary of "arms," "at fortune's alms" carries traces of "at fortune's hands."

18 See Eric Partridge, *Shakespeare's Bawdy* (New York, 1948): "*Pillicock male generative organs (pill,* 'testicle'; . . . *cock,* 'penis') and *Pillicock Hill the mount of Venus* + the *pudendum muliebre* . . ." Kenneth Muir notes that Florio gave "pillicock" for Italian *puga* ("penis").

19 "Proud" in "proud array" *means* "rich and splendid." Note, however, that in congenial contexts, *proud* was used to mean "lustful" (see *Venus and Adonis*, 260, where *proud* means "in heat"; compare *pride* in *Lucrece*, 705–06 and *Othello*, III.iii.404); *proud* was also used to mean "tumescent" (as in *Lucrece*, 712: "The flesh being proud, Desire doth fight with Grace"). See line 10 of sonnet 151.

20 For puns on *mad, maid, made*, see *Romeo and Juliet* III.ii.134–35, *Twelfth Night* III.iv.48–49, and Helge Kökeritz, *Shakespeare's Pronunciation* (New Haven, 1953), pp. 126, 164. If the actor who played Cordelia in I.i is a maid no longer—is now playing the Fool—then the Fool's exit speech reverberates in yet another extravagant direction.

21 The passage about crabapples, crustaceans, and mollusks appears to have generated from two proverbs that Shakespeare had on his mind when he was working on *The Taming of the Shrew:* "There's small choice in rotten apples" (I.i.132–33) and "He . . . doth resemble you . . . . As much as an apple doth an oyster" (IV.ii.99–101). The passage also continues and concludes a larger, though even more casual, incidental pattern in I.iv and I.v—a pattern of allusions to shells: see the Fool's offer to give Lear the two crowns of an egg (I.iv.149–57) and his reference to Lear as "a shealed peascod" (I.iv.190). That pattern, in turn, relates to substantial thematic common denominators that thread the play together—in particular, to the various assertions of the fact that, although shelter and clothing are necessary to us, they are not of the physical essence of human beings as they are of shelled creatures and are not to be counted on (not to be assumed and not to be trusted), and, more generally, the variously manifested fact that every kind of man-made protective, isolating shape and framework—physical or ideational—is transitory and frail.

22 Shakespeare's fascination with like-named but unlike characters is demonstrated in a long, mannered exchange in *Richard III:*

> *Queen Margaret.* . . . I had an Edward, till a Richard killed him;
> I had a Harry, till a Richard killed him:
> Thou hadst an Edward, till a Richard killed him;
> Thou hadst a Richard, till a Richard killed him.
> *Duchess of York.*
> I had a Richard too, and thou didst kill him . . .
>
> [IV.iv.40–44]

23 The traditionally probable and philosophically alarming consequences of dividing a kingdom never materialize in *King Lear*. In fact, the two wicked sisters immediately agree to act in unison, and—since their alliance is specifically formed to insure their father's subjection—we (like, I think, all audiences, even those weaned on Elizabethan political

philosophy) register their *union* as an instance of the evil Lear has loosed by dividing his kingdom between them. When Goneril and Regan do later fall out, their rivalry has no political ramifications: their armies fight as one against the French invaders.

24 An audience's incidental mental inconvenience in dealing with characters whose moment-to-moment behavior does not consistently conform to the identities the play dictates for them gets a casual echo when Regan protests a similar discrepancy between what she takes to be Lear's essential identity and the one implied by his manner: "I pray you, father, being weak, seem so" (II.iv.196). (Compare the correspondence between Oswald's complaint about Albany's responses ["What most he should dislike seems pleasant to him; / What like, offensive"— IV.ii.10–11] and a similar complaint that an audience could often make about its own.)

25 For an excellent account of the promised conflict between Albany and Cornwall and of the physics by which it acts as a red herring to the audience, see William H. Matchett's "Some Dramatic Techniques in *King Lear,*" in *Shakespeare: The Theatrical Dimension,* ed. Philip C. McGuire and David A. Samuelson (New York, 1979), pp. 185–208. Matchett's essay is generally illuminating and generally pertinent to this one. For example, his splendid analysis of the Gloucester-Edgar scenes in Act IV reveals the multifarious indefiniteness that surrounds Gloucester's attempt at suicide: Gloucester's accomplice in his failed suicide—a nonfinal final action—is the sane Edgar, who is pretending to be mad Tom and who seems for a while as if he may actually be about to behave insanely; we are not immediately certain but what Edgar plans to let Gloucester throw himself off a cliff—a cliff that is as real as a cliff can be on Shakespeare's bare stage and is, in fact, the only vividly described locale in the play.

Interlude

1 For a discussion of the generically comic elements in *Lear,* see Katharine Stockholder's "The Multiple Genres of *King Lear,*" *Bucknell Review* 16 (1968): 40–63; Stockholder's notes provide a useful working bibliography of earlier critical discussions of comedy in *Lear.* Also see Susan Snyder's *The Comic Matrix of Shakespeare's Tragedies* (Princeton, 1979).

2 Several other plays could have served my purposes here. For instance, indefinition is of the structural, dramatic, and intellectual essence of *Julius Caesar* and manifests itself even in the play's details. And the physics by which Beatrice's "Kill Claudio" (*Much Ado About Nothing,* IV.i.285) is both stunning and comic in its context are essentially those

that operate when Kent reminds Albany that he has forgotten the "great thing"—has forgotten about Lear and Cordelia.

For a more complex example, consider *All's Well That Ends Well*, a play with "end" in its title. In *All's Well* Shakespeare probes and harnesses the fact of generically ordained conclusion in a way precisely opposite to his way in *Lear*. In *All's Well* he activates the generic expectations pertinent to several different kinds of story: a "Griselda" plot—a secular saint's life—in which a virtuous heroine triumphs over adversities (adversities inflicted upon her by sticklike characters essentially motivated by the storyteller's desire to have severe and interesting trials for his saint to undergo), and in which the heroine, like Griselda and Helena ("My friends were poor but honest"—*All's Well That Ends Well*, I.iii.188), is marriageable but lowborn; a fairy tale in which a virtuous child is thwarted by a proud, insensitive stepmother figure (of the sort that the Countess resembles in I.iii ["Only sin / And hellish obstinacy tie thy tongue"—172−73], when we know she is in fact playing fairy godmother to Helena); a story about a young man led astray by an evil companion; a story about a young man married against his will to "a loathly lady"; a fairy tale in which a magically gifted young person is rewarded by a king who marries his benefactor to his own child; a "senex" plot, in which—to quote Grumio in *The Taming of the Shrew*—"to beguile the old folks . . . young folks lay their heads together" (I.ii.135−36). Shakespeare presses the promissory trappings of all these kinds of story into a single narrative and then—as if he did not see that they are incompatible—marches doggedly to a happy ending of a kind appropriate to any one of them but disconcertingly unsatisfying as a conclusion to the chimeralike play in which they coexist.

Shakespeare does something similar in *Two Gentlemen of Verona* where, in the last scene, Valentine follows the dictates of admirable, Platonic idealized friendship and not only performs his Christian duty by freely forgiving Proteus, the friend who has trespassed against him (forgiving too freely for the practical comfort of audiences, no matter how dedicated they may believe themselves to be to the theoretic requirements of Christian behavior), but also offers to "give" Proteus Silvia, the lady whose attractions occasioned the disruptive rivalry that has divided the two fast friends. Valentine and Shakespeare thus run roughshod over other culturally and emotionally sanctioned values that pertain to the view the play gives us of Valentine's, Proteus's, Silvia's, and Julia's situations—values ordinarily conveniently and carefully excluded from our perceptions of narratives that exemplify idealistically based action in order to recommend it to an audience.

3 For *catastrophe* meaning "end," see "The catastrophe is a nuptial" in

Armado's account of the story of the king and the beggarmaid (*Love's Labor's Lost* IV.i.76; Armado's next words introduce a play on *catastrophe* meaning "ruin"). Also note *2 Henry IV* II.i.56−57: "Away, you scullion! You rampallion! You fustilarian! I'll tickle your catastrophe [i.e., your arse]."

4 The issue of "issue"—of how events turn out—is a variously embodied common denominator of *King Lear* from its first moments, when Kent and Gloucester discuss their surprise that, although the King had always seemed to favor Albany over Cornwall, "now, in the division of the kingdom, it appears not which of the dukes he values most," and when, in their next exchange, they play on the word *issue* ("I cannot wish the fault undone, the issue of it being so proper"—I.i.16−17) during a discussion of the accidental birth of Edmund.

5 During the comparable sections of *Midsummer Night's Dream* I always worry about the discrepancies between Peter Quince's casting of "Pyramus and Thisbe" in I.ii and the performance he presents before the Duke—and I always feel silly for doing so. A similarly petty and similarly embarrassing thought process can intrude upon one's perception of *Love's Labor's Lost* if one notices that the portion of the pageant that we get to see only partially reflects the casting Holofernes proposes in the preceding scene. And, if one is a student of Shakespeare, one can catch oneself slipping into hopeless pettiness if one takes comfort from remembering that the Quarto and Folio texts of V.i.114−17, the speech in which Holofernes starts to distribute roles, is faulty. (The 1598 Quarto says, "Iosua, your selfe, my selfe, and this gallant Gentleman *Iudas Machabeus* . . . ." The Folio text is substantially the same.)

6 See Herbert A. Ellis, *Shakespeare's Lusty Punning in "Love's Labour's Lost"* (The Hague: Mouton, 1973), pp. 57−59, 125−27.

7 This kind of literally literary playfulness is still with us: in 1966 Eddy Arnold recorded a country-and-western song called "The Last Word in Lonesome Is Me." (In fact, most of the tricks and crotchets of Renaissance wit are still flourishing among the songwriters of Nashville.)

8 Costard appears to get from "enfranchise" to "enfrances me" to "marry me to one Frances" by hearing *en-* both as "one" ("one Frances") and—obscenely—as "in" ("in Frances me").

9 See Ellis, *Shakespeare's Lusty Punning,* pp. 52−54.

10 As the quatrain abruptly concluded by Berowne's line about greengeese is emblematic of the whole structure of *Love's Labor's Lost,* so in *All's Well That Ends Well* the Clown's all-purpose answer (II.ii.12−57)—an answer that "is like a barber's chair that fits all buttocks"—is emblematic of that play, which proceeds purposefully to a happy ending that could fit any one of the different generic shapes in the play but is not quite

satisfying as a conclusion to any one of them when they are pressed together in *All's Well*.

11 These lines are immediately followed by the entrance of Dumaine, the last of the four young men to enter the scene and declare his secret love. Berowne comments in an aside: "More sacks to the mill—O heavens, I have my wish! / Dumaine transformed—four woodcocks in a dish!" (IV.iii.76–77). Thus, this goose reference occurs, like the others, in a context where the completion of a foursome is at issue.

12 *OED*'s earliest example of *to goose*—a transitive verb meaning "to poke between the buttocks"—dates from the late nineteenth century (Supplement, 1972). Two contrasting factors of a goose's physique coincide in the verb: a powerfully thrusting neck and beak; a fat, sleek, soft body. Although the potential inherent in the contrast has always been there, the verb is not necessarily any older than *OED* says it is, but, on Shakespearean evidence alone, I strongly suspect that the noun *goose* was a slang synonym for the buttocks. Hilda Hulme—who, in *Explorations in Shakespeare's Language* (London, 1962; pp. 99–102), demonstrates Shakespearean allusion to *tailor* meaning "penis" and meaning "pudendum"—suggests that Puck's self-portrait (*A Midsummer Night's Dream*, II.i.42–57) alludes to a use of *tailor*—a word that includes the syllable *tail*—to mean "bum," "buttocks," and that, thus, the traditional folk practice of crying "tailor" when one falls suddenly and unexpectedly upon one's buttocks can be more simply and directly explained than it is by reference to the fact that tailors ordinarily sat cross-legged on the floor to sew. Tailors and geese are related in the term "tailor's goose" (a large pressing iron with a goose-neck-shaped handle). In *Macbeth*, the Porter welcomes an imaginary English tailor in out of the cold to warm himself: "Come in, tailor. Here you may roast your goose" (II.iii.13–14). The Porter presumably plays on "tailor's hell" (a nook under a tailor's shop-board into which shreds and scraps were thrown as perquisites of the tailor) and, considering the image of a man warming himself before a fire, may also pun on a sense of *goose* by which it meant "buttocks." Also consider the punning potential *goose* has in *Romeo and Juliet* II.iv.68–82, where the word appears in company with the word *wit*—which, among other things, meant both "penis" and "pudendum" (see Ellis, *Shakespeare's Lusty Punning*, pp. 103–10, 214–19):

> *Mercutio.* Nay, if our wits run the wild-goose
>   chase, I am done; for thou hast more of the wild
>   goose in one of thy wits than, I am sure, I have
>   in my whole five. Was I with you there for the
>   goose?

Romeo. Thou wast never with me for anything when
    thou wast not there for the goose.
Mercutio. I will bite thee by the ear for that
    jest.
Romeo. Nay, good goose, bite not!
Mercutio. Thy wit is a very bitter sweeting; it
    is a most sharp sauce.
Romeo. And is it not, then, well served in to a
    sweet goose?
Mercutio. O, here's a wit of cheveril, that
    stretches from an inch narrow to an ell broad!
Romeo. I stretch it out for that word 'broad,'
    which, added to the goose, proves thee far and
    wide a broad goose.

13 If—after the play is over (and presumably in response to the uncomplicated response I refer to)—one works *Love's Labor's Lost* over in one's
mind, one can complicate one's response by remembering that the
French king has been known to be "decrepit, sick, and bed-rid" since
scene i and that, ever since II.i.164, the Princess's party has been
specifically waiting for a messenger from the French court to arrive—or,
in more sophisticated fashion, by remembering that the very first lines of
the play concern death. However, I doubt anyone would argue that, at
the moment when Marcade arrives and delivers his news, an audience
thinks of those details from the play's dim past.

Part II

1 If a ninety-one-year-old man dies in his sleep on a Tuesday in March, we do
not call it a tragedy; if he dies at work on Friday morning of the week
before his annual two-week summer holiday, we are more likely to call it a
tragedy—more likely still if he is run over by his travel agent, and so on,
down to a nine-year-old boy violinist, dead of rosin poisoning on the stage
at Carnegie Hall on Christmas Eve.

2 In support of the proposition that lines 51–56 invite listeners to understand them to report combat between Macbeth and Cawdor—that the
syntactically, but *only* syntactically, obvious error *does* occur—I would
cite Roy Walker's *The Time Is Free* (London, 1949), pp. 19–23, 34–35.
Walker reviews the comments of earlier critics who have mistakenly taken
lines 53–56 to describe a fight between Macbeth and Cawdor, explains
the syntactic source of that error, *and then* points out a prospective irony in
the phrase "with self-comparisons," an irony that exists because—in the

words of the summary Kenneth Muir offers in a note on the phrase in his Arden edition (London, 1951; rev. ed., London and Cambridge, Mass., 1957)—"Macbeth is to match the Thane of Cawdor in treachery as well as in valour." Muir cites Walker's comment with apparent approval—an approval which I fully share, even though Walker's own carefully argued appeal to the syntactic logic of the lines shows Walker's point to be entirely misplaced. The fact that the lines cannot logically be understood to describe combat between Macbeth and Cawdor does not at all negate the fact that they are understood so. The bases and reality of the common misunderstanding of "him" in "Confronted him" are in fact very similar to those of the common and apparently valid understanding of "Bellona's bridegroom" as an epithet for Macbeth. That easy, usually instantaneous, and generally unchallenged equation derives, I suspect, from the fact that "Till that Bellona's *bridegroom* . . . *Confronted* him" echoes "Till *he* [Macbeth, valor's *minion*] *faced* the slave" in the Captain's first speech, a speech substantially parallel to this speech by Ross.

   It is presumably unnecessary here to add that the fact that, in the past, scholars of the "disintegrating" school have argued that the one surviving text for I.ii is, for one hypothetical reason or another, not what Shakespeare wrote, is irrelevant here because my topic is the play as we have it. Much the same is true of the fact that, as scholarly footnotes to student editions attest, many of the confusions in I.ii and some that follow from it (like Macbeth's surprising ignorance, in scene iii, of Cawdor's perfidy and disgrace), can be explained as accidents of Shakespeare's conflation of several incidents reported in Holinshed. Obviously, neither knowledge of, nor speculation on, the causes of such confusions does anything at all to remove them from an audience's experience of the play.

3 Context and logic dictate that "jump the life to come" be understood as "risk—take our chances with—the life to come" (for *to jump* meaning "to hazard," see *Cymbeline* V.iv.180−81: "jump the after-inquiry on your own peril"; for the related noun, see *Antony and Cleopatra* III.viii.5−6: "Our fortune lies / Upon this jump"). But the context of Macbeth's insistence upon location ("here, / But here"), and the eminently jumpable "bank and shoal" also activate the always commoner ordinary sense of *jump*: "leap." An understanding of *jump* as "risk" is likely always to have been a remedial afterthought, activated only if and when a listener is troubled by the physics of metaphors that seem to present simultaneous leaping and standing still.

4 Among lesser manifestations of the pattern in which pairs become trios, consider the variously lunatic hyperbole with which Macbeth responds when the witches intone his name three times in the apparition scene: "Had I three ears, I'ld hear thee" (IV.i.78), and the pregnant overtones to

Macbeth's theatre metaphor in "Two truths are told, / As happy prologues to the swelling act" (I.iii.127–28). Also note the complex increase on the verbal surface ("twofold . . . treble") and in the reported substance (the treble scepters are presumably the two traditionally used in English coronations plus the single scepter used in crowning Scottish kings at Scone) of the following clause from Macbeth's description of the show of future kings descended from Banquo: "and some I see / That twofold balls and treble sceptres carry" (IV.i.120–21—see Kenneth Muir's note in his Arden *Macbeth*).

5 See Bertrand Evans's chapter on *Macbeth* in *Shakespeare's Tragic Practice* (Oxford, 1979).

6 The first speech of the scene is Malcolm's "Let us seek out some desolate shade, and there / Weep our sad bosoms empty." Diana Lomont points out to me that that sentence invites audiences of this unusually quick-moving play to assume that Malcolm and Macduff already know about the final events of the preceding scene—that it is the massacre at Fife about which Malcolm proposes they weep their bosoms empty. Thus, since the generalness of the second sentence of Macduff's reply to Malcolm's proposal makes it evident that Macduff is still to hear of the events of the preceding scene, an audience can have active, personal experience of delay almost from the moment the scene begins. Note, moreover, that—in typically Shakespearean fashion—the lines that establish that Macduff has yet to hear the news do so in terms incidentally but urgently relevent to the facts of which they reveal their speaker's ignorance. Note *birthdom, New widows howl, new orphans cry,* and—still only moments after Lady Macduff has ceased her offstage cries—*yelled out* (in company with *Like,* which can momentarily say "similarly to"—even though it turns out to be an adjective):

> Let us rather
> Hold fast the mortal sword and, like good men,
> Bestride our downfall'n birthdom. Each new morn
> New widows howl, new orphans cry, new sorrows
> Strike heaven on the face, that it resounds
> As if it felt with Scotland and yelled out
> Like syllable of dolor.

[IV.iii.2–8]

7 In recent years several misguided directors have improved the plotline of *Macbeth* with interpolated stage business whereby one or more of the finally triumphant "virtuous" characters show questionable sides to themselves that Shakespeare never saw (for example, take the two most widely seen twentieth-century productions of *Macbeth,* the movie ver-

sions by Orson Welles and Roman Polanski; Welles had his Ross behave like a wicked medicine man from a Western, and Polanski added a Richard III-like Donalbain who returned to Scotland to skulk about registering evil intent in dumbshow). I suggest that, though such interpolations are purely, foolishly, and destructively creative, the interpolators did respond to elements that are powerful and real in the play—in the *play,* but not in the story it tells us. The "good" characters and their scenes are the villains of *Macbeth*—of the play *as* play. They are, however, no more the villains of the dramatized sequence of events than they have previously seemed to be.

8 The play's demands for attention to Siward would, I think, have been a nuisance to a Jacobean audience, even if—as I suspect may have been the case (see Appendix 2)—the role of Siward was taken by the actor who previously played Banquo, and whose appearance as Siward could have suggested the then most interesting particular of the supposed destiny of Banquo's line—that, in 1603, with the succession of James VI of Scotland as James I of England, Banquo's supposed issue would unite the island under one rule.

9 "Each way and move" is the Folio reading. The Pelican text, following Dover Wilson's reasonable but arbitrary and unnecessary emendation, reads "Each way and none." The emendation diminishes the passage by removing a sort of semantic onomatopoeia that the final sentence gets from coming firmly to precise syntactic rest on the infinite aimlessness of "and move."

10 When I say that a phenomenon goes unobserved by audiences, my authority is usually the scholarly commentators who have—have triumphantly—observed it: what is worth revealing needs revelation, is not immediately apparent.

Appendix 2

1 Compare the last scene of Jonson's *Epicoene* where a member of a boy company playing an adult male snatched away Epicoene's wig so that a stage full of boy actors playing characters of all ages and sexes could see for themselves that Epicoene is not a woman but a boy. Shakespeare, writing for an adult company, exploits similar metaphysics in the induction of *The Taming of the Shrew,* when he presents an actor playing a boy dressed as Christopher Sly's lady and then presents a group of male actors playing male actors who play men and women in a story that focuses on real and imagined distinctions between masculine and feminine behavior.

2 The early evidence is well presented and sensibly discussed in David

Bevington's *From Mankind to Marlowe* (Cambridge, Mass., 1962). On the subject of doubling on the London stage during Shakespeare's professional lifetime, see W. W. Greg, *Dramatic Documents from the Elizabethan Playhouses,* 2 vols. (Oxford, 1931), and the studies by William J. Lawrence, Alwin Thaler, and William A. Ringler, Jr., cited below.

3 At American county fairs it always used to take a brave and highly skilled master of ceremonies to quiet an audience and focus its attention long enough to begin an open-air program in daylight. The men I remember had trouble, even though they had loudspeakers and little brass bands to help them. Moreover, audiences at county fairs always doubted that the Hollywood star (perhaps the former comical sidekick to a singing cowboy) was actually there as advertised. The same conditions now obtain at supermarket openings and, in the mid-1960s, developed in the face of the awesome technological credentials of national television. The Beatles were to appear on *The Ed Sullivan Show;* the studio audience would not quiet down for the supporting acts that led up to the star turn next-to-closing. When the Beatles were scheduled again, Sullivan did what MCs do at county fairs and suburban supermarkets: he showed the Beatles to the audience for a minute at the beginning, and the audience, assured that it would get what it came for, sat with reasonable patience through forty preliminary minutes of nightclub comics and dancing mice.

  Shakespeare may have created Francisco, Archidamus, and Philo, characters who speak the opening lines of their plays and never appear after scene i, for the specific purpose of allowing Burbage or an actor of similar stature to quiet the audience by his talent and, perhaps, reassure them by his presence.

4 William A. Ringler, Jr., "The Number of Actors in Shakespeare's Early Plays," in *The Seventeenth-Century Stage,* ed. Gerald Eades Bentley (Chicago, 1968), pp. 110–34. Ringler says that *A Midsummer Night's Dream* has "four women characters who cannot double—Helena, Hermia, Titania, and Hippolyta (Helena, Hermia, and Titania are on stage together at IV, 1:1; and though Titania exits at [101] while the other two remain, Hippolyta immediately enters at [102], so none of these four parts can be doubled)" (p. 133). By Ringler's logic, Oberon (who exits with Titania at IV.i.101), and Theseus (who enters with Hippolyta at 102), could not be doubled either.

5 London, 1952: rev. ed., London and Cambridge, Mass., 1957, p. 217. Muir properly ignores a possible line of argument based on a rather new but well-entrenched tradition that says Robert Armin played Lear's Fool (and would not have played the obvious boy's role of Cordelia); there is

no evidence whatever that Armin played Lear's Fool (nor, of course, is there any proof that he did not).

6 Of plays printed during Shakespeare's career, the only other known distribution tables occur in the 1598 and 1610 quartos of *Mucedorus*. They are incomplete and less interesting than the one in *The Fair Maid of the Exchange,* but, for the parts they do distribute, they are workable. See Lawrence, *Pre-Restoration Stage Studies* (Cambridge, Mass., 1927), pp. 58–59.

7 The doubling of Duncan and Macduff is possible if one takes the Folio's opening stage direction for I.vi *(Enter King, Malcolm, Donalbaine, Banquo, Lenox, Macduff, Rosse, Angus, and Attendants)* as a literary embellishment. Only Duncan, Banquo, and Lady Macbeth speak in I.vi. Moreover, the stage directions in early texts are notoriously casual and notoriously independent of physical necessities dictated in dialogue. Still, it is well to remember that the doubling of Duncan and Macduff can be conjectured only if one allows oneself the arbitrary luxury of ignoring stage directions that indicate the presence of a character who does not speak and is not mentioned in the dialogue as being present.

The same liberty allows—and casts doubt on—the inviting possibility that the actor who appeared as the shipmaster in I.i. of *The Tempest* played Prospero thereafter. The master, who is the first character to speak in *The Tempest,* exits after his second speech and never speaks again. The master has Prospero-like superiority, both metaphorically —in his office—and literally—in that the fourth speech of the play suggests that the master is then on an upper stage, invisible to the boatswain and mariners but visible to the audience (that speech also generates an incidentally suggestive confusion between the master and the storm):

> *Boatswain.*   Heigh, my hearts! Cheerly, cheerly, my
> hearts! Yare, yare! Take in the topsail! Tend to th'
> master's whistle! Blow till thou burst thy wind,
> if room enough!
>
> > [I.i.5–8]

But Prospero specifically lists the master as one of the two mariners he sends Ariel to fetch in V.i (97–101), and the stage direction at line 216 calls for Ariel, the boatswain, and the master to enter. Still, the master has no lines in Act V, and the boatswain speaks of him in a manner appropriate to someone not then onstage (the *we* of the boatswain's last sentence could refer to any token mariner brought on with the boatswain and chosen from the mute supernumeraries who appear as mariners in I.i):

Boatswain.

. . . .

We were awaked; straightway at liberty;
Where we, in all her trim, freshly beheld
Our royal, good, and gallant ship, our master
Cap'ring to eye her. On a trice, so please you,
Even in a dream, were we divided from them
And were brought moping hither.

[V.i.235—40]

8 Here again, there is genuine but inconclusive evidence against the possibility I propose: Paris's dying words to Romeo are, "Open the tomb, lay me with Juliet" (V.iii.73); Romeo says he will do so, and then apparently does ("lie thou there, by a dead man interred"—87). In modern productions, Romeo never takes "with Juliet" to mean "alongside"; he reserves that place for his own corpse; in most productions Paris's body is dragged to the rear and is often actually invisible when Friar Lawrence says, "Thy husband in thy bosom there lies dead; / And Paris too" (155—56). The lines make my suggestion less probable, but they do not make it impossible.

9 Since all of this is so obviously speculative, it may be unnecessary to note that the doublings I suggest are not the only ones that could be proposed. For instance, the case for one actor playing the phonetic triplets Archidamus, Antigonus, and Autolycus is at least as good as the one for doubling Antigonus and Camillo; as Northrop Frye has shown us (in *A Natural Perspective* [New York, 1965], p. 115), Antigonus's shoulder-bone (III.iii.91) and Autolycus's shoulder-blade (IV.iii.71) join the two like Siamese twins.

10 Note that "sur-addition" contains the sound of "Sir"—a post-Roman British counterpart of honorary epithets like "Leonatus"—and that "Leonatus" contains the idea of birth—the general and specific topic of this speech on Posthumus's "name and birth," a speech in which "So gained the sur-addition Leonatus" is an urgently nonessential incidental detail, a sur-addition by a garrulous gossip.

11 In this context there is hardly need to mention that the five actors needed to play the five characters in Posthumus's dream (V.iv.30—122) are likely candidates for doubling and that the play itself points to actors whose use in those parts would underscore rhymelike contrasts and/or equations: Guidarius and Arviragus as the Leonati; the Queen (Cloten's mother) as Posthumus's mother; Cymbeline (or Belarius) as Posthumus's father; and Belarius (or Cymbeline) as Jupiter.

12 I am also tempted to speculate on the potential in the plays for a related

phenomenon: allusion by means of casting in one play to the casting of another play previously in the company's repertory or still in it.

Consider, for instance, the mental fireworks to be had from the distribution of roles in *Romeo and Juliet* among members of a company that also regularly presented *A Midsummer Night's Dream*. Or consider the posthumous commentary on Hotspur (who, though parodied by the blowhard Douglas, dies still noble and attractive to the audience of *1 Henry IV*) that would have been inherent in a production of *2 Henry IV* where the actor who played Hotspur in one play played Pistol (and, perhaps, Rumor) in the other.

Or consider the presumably nonjudgmental but casually and theatrically enlivening potential inherent in a repertory that contained *Love's Labor's Lost,* the Falstaff plays, *Julius Caesar,* and *Hamlet*. In his misdelivered letter to Jaquenetta (*Love's Labor's Lost* IV.i.61–86), Don Armado makes a comically inappropriate, comically complex equation among himself, Julius Caesar, and King Cophetua ("he it was that might rightly say veni, vidi, vici"). Falstaff compares himself to Julius Caesar: "I may justly say, with the hook-nosed fellow of Rome . . . 'I came, saw, and overcame' " (*2 Henry IV,* IV.iii.39–41); and the Host of the Garter, whose humor it is to heap meaningless variety of honorific, vaguely classical epithets on Falstaff and the rest of his acquaintances, says that Falstaff is "an emperor—Caesar, Keiser, and Pheazar" (*The Merry Wives of Windsor,* I.iii.9). Polonius played Caesar "once i' th' university":

> *Polonius.* I did enact Julius Caesar. I was
>   killed i' th' Capital; Brutus killed me.
> *Hamlet.* It was a brute part of him to kill
>   so capital a calf
>
>   [*Hamlet* III.ii.99–102]

Two scenes later, Hamlet—very possibly played by the actor who played Brutus in Shakespeare's *Julius Caesar*—kills Polonius and lugs "the guts into the neighbor room." If an actor regularly cast as Shakespeare's Julius Caesar (who, like Plutarch's, wants the men about him to be fat), took one or more of the other three parts—Armado, Falstaff, or Polonius—the incidental, substantively irrelevant energy would have been theatrically powerful (as similarly but less precisely allusive casting has been in our own times when Bing Crosby and Frank Sinatra were cast as priests, when a German music-hall clown played Hermann Göring in a serious historical film about World War II, when Peter Sellers played Richard III, and when George Rose played Julius Caesar).

Lest anyone fear that I take any one of these *particular* purely speculative examples as more than speculative, let me make it clear that, though I take the idea of intercourse between plays very seriously as a theatrical phenomenon, the possibilities for doubling presented in this note are, like those in the body of the essay, presented only *as* possibilities, illustrative possibilities. If there were a way to test such speculations as these, I would not, for example, be surprised to hear that Shakespeare's company had an enormously fat actor who played Falstaff and, in *Hamlet,* played not Polonius but Claudius, whose physial grossness is often suggested overtly ("the bloat king"—III.iv.183) and by implication ("Your fat king and your lean beggar is but variable service"—IV.iii.23—24).

13 If the need for tentativeness were not self-evident, it would be made so by the fact that the altogether improbable reader who accepted *all* my suggested doubles would thereby find himself obliged to imagine the actor who played Falstaff also playing Octavius in *Julius Caesar*. To imagine that unlikely but not impossible double probably requires greater liberation from modern theatrical assumptions than is either attainable or advisable.

AN INDEX OF SHAKESPEAREAN PLAYS,
SCENES, AND LINES DISCUSSED

The index sometimes sacrifices scholarly nicety to efficiency. The parenthetical words after act, scene, and line numbers are there to identify the cited passages quickly. Where the tag phrase is a scrap of Shakespearean text, it is not always the first phrase of the cited passage; often it is a more distinctive phrase from the body of the cited passage, a phrase more likely to recall to a reader just which passage it is the numbers refer to.

All's Well That Ends Well, 166n
  II.ii.12–57 (the Clown's
    all-purpose answer), 167n,
    168n
Antony and Cleopatra, 130–31,
    142–44, 173n
As You Like It, 131, 155
  I.ii.106–07 ("There comes an
    old man . . ."), 161n
The Comedy of Errors, 153n
Cymbeline, 149–53, 155, 175n
Hamlet, 124–25, 130–31, 136,
    139, 173n, 176n, 177n
Henry IV, Part One, 131, 141, 176n
Henry IV, Part Two, 131, 141–42,
    176n
Henry V, 129–31
Julius Caesar, 130–31, 135, 140,
    165n, 176n, 177n
  I.i.35 ("You blocks, you stones
    . . ."), 162n
  III.ii.142 ("You are not wood,
    you are not stones . . ."), 162n
King Lear, 1–57, 61–62, 65,
    73–74, 78, 121–22,

    124–25, 129, 134–35,
    153–54, 159n–165n, 167n,
    173n, 174n
  I.i.1–2 ("more affected the
    Duke of Albany than
    Cornwall"), 56, 165n, 167n
  I.i.7–32 (Edmund's
    bastardizing), 56, 167n
  I.i.41 ("Unburdened crawl
    toward death"), 17
  I.i.62 ("What shall Cordelia
    speak? . . ."), 54
  I.i.69–70 ("I am made of that
    same mettle . . ."), 45
  I.i.101–05 ("But goes thy heart
    with this? . . ."), 13
  I.i.107 ("So young, my lord, and
    true"), 54
  I.i.121–39 ("between the
    dragon and his wrath"),
    14–15
  I.i.130–39 ("I do invest you
    jointly . . ."), 14
  I.i.145–49, 155–57 (Kent's
    honorable insolence), 51

King Lear (continued)

I.i.223−33 ("I yet beseech your Majesty . . ."), 55

I.i.268−75, 280−82 ("The jewels of our father . . . Cordelia leaves you"), 55

I.i.276 ("Prescribe not us our duty"), 55

I.i.283−306 (Goneril and Regan discuss their new circumstances), 45, 54

I.ii.101−12 ("These late eclipses . . ."), 49−50

I.ii.130−31 ("like the catastrophe of the old comedy"), 55, 62

I.iv.9−21, 30−41 (Kent auditions to join Lear's retinue), 38−39, 154

I.iv.55−63 ("your Highness is not entertained with that ceremonious affection"), 50−51

I.iv.68−78 ("But where's my fool? . . ."), 154

I.iv.90 ("Let me hire him too . . ."), 39, 154

I.iv. 144−48 ("This is not altogether fool . . ."), 37, 39

I.iv.254 ("My train are men of choice and rarest parts"), 50

I.iv.266−301 (Lear curses Goneril), 17

I.iv.306−12 ("Nuncle Lear . . . So the fool follows after"), 39−40

I.v.12−28 (the *crab/apple* passage), 43−45

I.v.28−46 ("Thou wouldst make a good fool"), 38, 76

I.v.45−46 ("She that's a maid . . . and laughs . . ."), 38−40, 164n

II.ii.1−17 (Oswald and Kent before Gloucester's castle), 51−52

II.ii.41−42 (Kent challenges Edmund), 52

II.iii.21 ("Edgar I nothing am"), 46

II.iv.50−51 ("Fortune that arrant whore . . ."), 161n

II.iv. 84−184 (Lear's confrontation with Regan), 17−18

II.iv.196 ("being weak, seem so"), 165n

III.i.4 - III.iv (Lear in the storm), 18−20, 161n

III.ii.74−96 ("He that has and a little tiny wit" and the Fool's prophecy), 40−43

III.iv.9−11 ("Thou'dst shun a bear . . ."), 57

III.iv.68−79 ("Nothing could have subdued nature / To such a lowness . . . Pillicock sat on Pillicock hill . . ."), 35−37

III.iv.75 ("fools and madmen"), 37

III.iv.80−95, 118−32 (Poor Tom), 39

III.iv.173−75 (Child Rowland . . ."), 39

III.vi.83 ("And I'll go to bed at noon"), 163n

III.vii.73 ("I have served you . . . since I was a child"), 46

IV.i.1−26 ("Yet better thus . . ."), 13−14

IV.ii.10−11 ("What most he should dislike . . ."), 47, 113, 165n

IV.iii.1−6 ("Why the King of France is . . . gone back . . ."), 153

IV.iv.23−24 ("It is thy business that I go upon"), 161n

IV.vi (Gloucester at Dover Cliff and his meeting with Lear), 18, 165n

IV.vii (Lear's meeting with Cordelia), 18

IV.vii.61 ("Fourscore and upward . . ."), 13

IV.vii.96−97 ("My point and period . . ."), 6

V.i.34−37 ("I know the riddle"), 122

V.ii.11 ("Ripeness is all. . . . And that's true too."), 22

V.ii.89 ("An interlude!"), 55−56

V.iii.22−25 ("Help, help! O help . . ."), 10, 23

V.iii.38−39 ("I cannot draw a cart . . ."), 22

V.iii.40−66 (Albany, Goneril, Regan, and Edmund bickering), 6−7

V.iii.171−74 ("The gods are just . . ."), 7, 47

V.iii.176−222 (Edgar's narrative), 8−9, 11−12, 154

V.iii.230 ("Here comes Kent"), 9

V.iii.235−37 ("Great thing of us forgot!"), 9, 16

V.iii.244−52 ("Quickly send . . . to the castle"), 10−11

V.iii.258−316 (Lear over the body of Cordelia and Edgar over Lear's), 23−33, 154

V.iii.275−79 ("I killed the slave that was a-hanging thee . . ."), 28−29

V.iii.279−95 ("Who are you? . . . Are you not Kent? . . . Where is your servant Caius? . . ."), 30−32

V.iii.281−82 ("If Fortune brag of two . . ."), 30

V.iii.297−305 (Albany resigns his power "during the life of this old Majesty" and promises justice), 25−28

V.iii.306 ("And my poor fool is hanged"), 32−33, 129, 163n

V.iii.312−27 ("Look there, look there . . ."), 15−16, 57

Love's Labor's Lost, 61−78, 139, 148−49, 166n−169n, 176n

I.i.94−99 ("green geese are a-breeding"), 71−72

I.i.130−34 (Jaquenetta's snappy answers), 64

I.i.220−23 (Costard completes the King's sentences), 64

I.ii.34−52 ("I have promised to study three years . . ."), 66−67

III.i.63−123 (Costard's broken shin), 68−70, 72

IV.i.76 ("The catastrophe is a nuptial"), 166n, 167n

IV.ii.69−70 ("A green goose a goddess"), 72

V.i.69 ("Thou hast it ad dunghill . . ."), 73

V.i.91−94 ("dally with my excrement"), 73

V.i.114−17 (proposed cast list for the Worthies pageant), 64−65, 167n

V.ii.13−15 (Katharine's dead sister), 67, 75

V.ii.15−46 (the ladies' set of wit), 67

V.ii.158−68 ("*Enter . . . the boy, with a speech* . . ."), 64

V.ii.219−20 ("Since you are strangers and come here by

Love's Labor's Lost (*continued*)
chance . . ."), 61–62, 125

V.ii.485–704 (the pageant of
the Nine Worthies), 65–68,
73

V.ii.617–20 (Jude–ass), 73

V.ii.621 ("This is not generous
. . ."), 67–68, 75

V.ii.705–11 (*"Enter . . .
Marcade . . ."*), 63, 124

V.ii. 864–68 ("Our wooing
doth not end . . ."), 62, 76

Macbeth 81, 86, 90–118, 131,
140, 169n–172n, 174n

I.i.11 ("Fair is foul . . ."),
117–18

I.ii.7–62 (battle narratives by
the bleeding soldier and Ross),
96–101

I.iii.43–47 ("You should be
women"), 102

I.iii.58–63 ("If you can look
into the seeds of time . . ."),
101

I.iii.127–28 ("Two truths are
told . . ."), 171n

I.iv. 28–29 ("I have begun to
plant thee . . ."), 91–92

I.iv.35–43 ("The Prince of
Cumberland"), 91

I.v.52–59 (Lady Macbeth greets
Macbeth), 95

I.vi.1–10 ("This castle hath a
pleasant seat . . ."), 106

I.vii.1–28 ("If it were done
when 'tis done . . ."), 103–05

II.iii.13–14 ("Come in tailor
. . ."), 168n

II.iii.96 ("Your royal father's
murdered . . ."), 107

II.iii.115–16 ("Why do we hold
our tongues . . ."), 107

III.iv. 78–80 ("when the brains

were out, the man would
die"), 94

IV.i.49 ("a deed without a
name"), 118

IV.i.78 ("Had I three ears . . ."),
170n

IV.i.120–21 ("twofold balls and
treble scepters"), 171n

IV.iii (Malcolm, Macduff, and
Ross in England), 106–11,
171n

V.ii ("Near Birnam Wood / Shall
we well meet them"),
111–12

V.iv ("Let every soldier hew him
down a bough"), 111–12

V.v.17–28 ("To-morrow, and
to-morrow . . ."), 94–96

V.vi ("Your leavy screens throw
down"), 111–12

V.viii.33–34 ("Lay on, Macduff
. . ."), 92–93

V.viii. 39–47 (the death of
young Siward), 93

V.viii. 60–75 (the last speech),
91–92

The Merry Wives of Windsor, 176n

A Midsummer Night's Dream,
131–34, 139, 167n, 176n

Much Ado about Nothing, 165n,
166n

Othello, 122–23, 153n

Richard II, 140–41

Richard III

IV.iv.40–44 ("till a Richard
killed him"), 164n

Romeo and Juliet, 142, 175n, 176n

II.iv, 68–82 ("our wits run the
wild-goose chase"), 168n,
169n

The Taming of the Shrew, 172n

I.i.132–33 ("small choice in
rotten apples"), 164n

IV.ii.99−101 ("as much as an
apple doth an oyster"), 164n
The Tempest, 124, 174n, 175n
Troilus and Cressida
I.iii.125−34 (Ulysses' speech on
"degree"), 48
Twelfth Night, 130, 147−48
The Two Gentlemen of Verona, 166n
The Winter's Tale, 131, 146−47,
173n, 175n

Al